The
Little Mac
Book

SECOND EDITION

Robin Williams

Kay Nelson

Peachpit Press
Berkeley ▾ California

The Little Mac Book second edition
© 1990, 1991 by Robin Williams and Kay Nelson
  (previously published under the title *Macintosh Basics; An informal guide to using the Mac,* by Performance Enhancement Products)

Peachpit Press
2414 Sixth Street
Berkeley, California 94710
415.527.8555
415.548.5991 fax

Notice of Liability

Trademarks

ISBN 0-938151-68-1

0 9 8 7 6 5 4 3 2
Printed and bound in the United States of America

To my mother, Patricia Williams,
who made it possible,
and to my father, Gerald Williams,
who would have been proud.

Acknowledgments

I must thank Brad Mager for insisting that—
as an instructor of graphic design—
I not be computer-illiterate, thus leading me
into the exciting new field of electronic design;
Dwight Tracy for being my kind conspirator
in the acquisition of my first Macintosh;
Alex Drake, for so patiently answering
my interminable questions over the past few years;
Marilyn Flowers, Shirley Davis, and particularly
Richard Abrahams and Roger Karraker,
for their warm support and encouragement;
all my students, for whom this was originally prepared;
and Beverly Scherf and Mary Boston,
for taking care of so many of the details of life.

For this second edition, I heartily thank
Kay Yarborough Nelson for providing me
with the information for the chapters on System 7.
Kay wrote the highly-acclaimed *Little System 7 Book,*
which is *the* book to get if you really want
to reach into the depths of System 7.

And thanks to Richard Theriault
for his gentle and humorous,
yet very constructive and valuable critiques;
Andrew Wynn Rouse, for sharing his System 7 expertise
with such alacrity;
and dear Mary Grady, for compiling the index for me
so quickly, yet so thoroughly.

Contents

> In this work, when it shall be found that much is omitted, let it not be forgotten that much likewise is performed.
>
> —Dr. Samuel Johnson, upon completion of his dictionary, 1755

Part I ▾ Macintosh Basics

Part II ▾ System 7

PART ONE

READ ME FIRST

The Concept

I hope you were warned, before you ever invested in a Macintosh, that this little computer is addictive. It pulls you in. It has you inventing work for yourself just so you can use it. It creates an attitude that makes you feel like you're having fun while being productive—what a concept.

There's not much you need to know to operate the Mac. That's why this book is so little. This book is just a direct path to the essentials of operating the computer so you can get straight to the fun, I mean *work*, without wasting too much time diddling around trying to figure it out. There's not much technical information here because most of us don't need it or want it; you don't have to know how to fly the plane to take a vacation in Paris.

System 6 or 7

There is one technical point that I do have to note right here, though. Please forgive me. This edition of *The Little Mac Book* comes at an awkward time in the evolution of the Macintosh. You have probably heard some of the hoopla about System 7, the new "operating system" (see page 11) that runs the computer. For the next year or so some people will be working with System 7 and many people will continue working with previous versions (hopefully some version of System 6). Even if you don't quite understand what an "operating system" is, you should know whether you are using System 7 or not. There is an instant way to tell: Look in the upper right corner of your screen when the Mac is on. If you see a little question mark inside a balloon-like thing, your computer is "running" System 7.

If you see this icon, or picture, in the upper right of your screen, your Mac is using System 7.

Most of the basic functions in both Systems operate exactly the same; System 7 just has a few new bells and whistles. Since most people are still using System 6, the major portion of this book is written from that standpoint. Chapters 23 through 30 relate specifically to System 7. Wherever you see this symbol, ▽, in the first portion of the book, it means that particular feature is a little different in System 7. If you are running System 6, ignore that little symbol. If you are running System 7, you should probably check out the referenced pages to note the difference.

I apologize for any awkwardness this combination of System 6 and System 7 may present, but we just have to accept the fact that things will be awkward for a while until the dust settles and we all get back on an even footing.

If technical information really bothers you, skip the first chapter—you can live without it for a while. That chapter isn't as painful as it sounds, actually, but if you're a little nervous about using a computer in the first place, just bounce right over to the second chapter, called "Starting Up." In fact, skip over anything that doesn't make sense right away. That's one of the most wonderful things about the Mac—we can bumble along for a long time on just a little bit of information. When your brain is ready to absorb more, come back to the parts that didn't make sense the first time around. The information will still be there.

Whenever you come across a term you are not familiar with, check the index. It will refer you to the page where that term is defined.

Anyway, technical stuff aside, I do hope you have fun and take advantage of this new concept in productivity as you, too, become addicted.

CHAPTER ONE

Ks, Megs, and Disks

People who've been working with the Mac for a while start tossing around jargon like, "It won't fit cuz it's a 900K document," or "My SE has 30 megs," and people who are not familiar with the Mac feel dumb because it all sounds so esoteric and we're sure we'll never be able to understand all this sophisticated computer stuff and besides we don't want to know all that technical stuff anyway we just want to learn how to run the darn thing. Well, as far as technical stuff goes, all most of us need to know is the machine is magic. Pure, simple, magic. Like an airplane.

Knowing the difference between a bit and a byte and a K and a meg, though, can help organize things in your brain a little bit so what you are working with will make more sense. This is how it goes:

Actually, the computer isn't that smart; it can only count to one. Remember in school when we learned the binary system, which we have now completely forgotten about, except that for some reason you could only count from zero to one and you had to use exponential notation? Well, Mac uses a binary system: it counts zero and one— zero means Off and one means On. See, it sends these little electronic messages, each a series of Off and On. And each one of those little messages is a **bit.**

Now, one little bit doesn't tell the computer a whole lot, so it strings together a bunch of bits to create a more important message: eight bits, such as **01000001,** makes one **byte.** As you can see in the column to the right, one byte of information is still rather limited— it takes a lot of bytes to create any sort of document.

So a bunch of bytes is grouped together and called a **kilobyte.** You would think that a kilobyte would be a thousand bytes, yes? No. Since the computer can only count to one, the closest it can get to 1000 in its binary system with exponential notation is 1024. But we generally round it off and say there's about 1000 bytes in a kilobyte. And kilobytes are the **K**s everyone talks about.

Technical Magic

Bits

0 1

Each one of these is one bit

Bytes

01000001

This byte represents the letter A.

Kilobytes

Approximately 1000 Bytes equals 1 Kilobyte.

How do Ks figure in real life? Kilobytes are what disk space and file/document size are measured in; the larger and more sophisticated the document or the software program, the greater the number of K it will occupy on the disk.

Floppy Disks

You've probably seen the nice little 3.5" **floppy disks** that the Mac uses. A disk stores the information for running the computer, for operating the programs, for saving the documents you create. Originally the Mac could only deal with a single-sided disk (one that took information on only one side of itself), but unless you have a very old machine with only a single-sided drive, you won't be using single-sided disks.

Disk Capacity

A **normal double-sided disk** holds about **800K** (kilobytes) of data. Four pages of double-spaced typewritten text takes about 6K of disk space; therefore, you can get about *500 pages* of textual information on one disk (leaving some room for the messages it has to send to the computer). Spreadsheets, graphics, and other complex info take up a lot more space, of course.

High-density disks have an extra hole on the right side of the disk.

A **high-density double-sided disk** holds about **1.4MB** (megabytes, which are bigger than kilobytes, see page 10) of data. These disks look just like normal disks, except they usually have the letters HD somewhere on them, and they have an extra hole. That extra hole tells the Mac that the disk is high-density; only Macs with a "SuperDrive" (like the SE30, the Mac II family, and the LC) can read these high-density disks. Some people advocate putting a piece of tape over the extra hole to trick other Macs into reading the disk, but that almost always ends in a disk failure. Don't risk your work.

Caring for Floppy Disks

Why is the disk called a floppy disk when it's not floppy? Actually, it is floppy. If you slide over that metal end you'll see the floppy disk inside. Don't touch it! It's full of tiny messages that your oily fingers or sharp nails can destroy. Keep your disks away from heat: they'll warp just like a record album when left in your hot car. And keep them away from magnets—a magnet will destroy all the data on the disk. So don't attach them to your refrigerator; don't store them near your telephone or stereo or any other electronic device; and don't pile them on top of your magnetic paperclip holder.

I also recommend you don't keep disks in those little plastic bags they often come in; the plastic can build up static electricity which has the potential to destroy your precious data.

When you buy your floppy disks, they aren't *formatted* and so must be **initialized.** They come unformatted because other types of computers are now using these handy little things, and they can be initialized for either type. So when you first insert an uninitialized disk, Mac asks you several questions. You need to name the disk and you need to choose to initialize it single-sided or double-sided. Obviously, if it's a double-sided disk you'll choose double-sided. The system may warn you that you are going to erase all the information on the disk, but since it's blank, so what. When you finally click OK, the Mac will lay down the formatting it needs to store all the valuable info you will be giving it.

It is possible to **lock** a disk. When a disk is locked, whoever is using it cannot change anything on it, nor can other files be saved onto it. To lock a disk, find the little black tab in the corner. You'll notice you can slide it up or down.

▾ When the tab covers the hole, the disk is unlocked.

▾ When you can see through the hole, the disk is locked.

A **hard disk** is actually a large, *hard disk*, rather than a floppy piece of film. In principle it works the same as a floppy disk, but it can hold a great deal more data. The hard disk itself can be installed inside your Mac, or it may be a separate unit. Either way, a hard disk is a storage container for holding all your documents and software applications, and typically holds your *System Folder* for starting your machine (see page 11 for more info on the System Folder). Hard disks allow you to store your applications and documents all on one disk instead of on a lot of separate floppies, making it *much* easier and faster to work. It is essential now to have a hard disk, as applications and documents are rapidly outgrowing even the double-sided disks.

Initializing a New Disk

Locking a Disk

This disk is unlocked.

Hard Disks

Megabytes

Approximately 1000 K equals one Megabyte.

In fact, a hard disk holds so much data that it's not even measured in kilobytes; it's measured in **megabytes,** also known as **megs** or **MB.** You've already figured out that one megabyte is 1024 kilobytes, right? Right.

Now, 1024 kilobytes (one megabyte) is more than what *one* normal floppy disk can hold. Hard disks come in various sizes, able to store from 20 megs to 30 to 80 to 160 megs of information, and they're getting bigger all the time. So on a small hard disk then, say 20 megs, you have as much storage space as on *more than 25 floppy disks!* You can load all kinds of applications onto your hard disk and create all kinds of documents without having to fiddle with putting floppies in and out. As the software applications get more and more sophisticated, they take up more and more space, and already there are applications that just can't be used without a hard disk.

Make Back up Disks

Always **back up** your software applications. As soon as you buy a new application, make a copy of all the disks and **use the copy** (the *copy* is your back up); keep the original disks safe in a clean, dust-free place. That way if a catastrophe happens to befall your application that you paid so much money for, you always have an extra copy. Software companies, you know, won't give you a new copy if you destroy yours.

Also always make sure you have a current back up copy of *everything* on your hard disk—all your documents you have so laboriously created. A hard disk can "crash" and leave no survivors. At the end of each working day, or more often if it is really important, make copies (page 37) onto disks of everything you created or modified that day (label the disks!).

You certainly don't want to lose all that data. A hard disk comes with a back up application—be sure to check it out. If you are in a situation where there are massive amounts of information to back up regularly, check into those applications designed specifically for the process.

Rule Number 3

Back Up Often. Like everyday.

(No, you didn't miss Rules 1 and 2—Rule 1 is on page 51; Rule 2 is on page 44.)

CHAPTER TWO

STARTING UP

The Mac turns on with a little switch on the back left of the machine—admittedly a very inconvenient place. A Mac II, though, can also be turned on with either the big key with the triangle on it at the top of the SE keyboard (that key that is useless for everybody else), or the key on the top far right on the extended keyboard. It's recommended on a Mac II that you always use the keyboard for turning it on and off, rather than the switch on the back.

If you have an *internal hard disk* for your machine, as soon as you turn it on it will **boot up** from the System on the hard disk. (The term "boot up" comes from the idea of pulling itself up by its bootstraps, as the Mac is going into its own System and turning itself on.)

If you have an *external hard disk*, that piece of hardware should be turned on first, and then turn on your Mac.

If your computer has *any other switches* for turning it on, either on top of the monitor or on the keyboard, the switch on the back of the Macintosh must always be turned on as well (see page 93).

If you don't have a hard disk (you can read a little about hard disks on page 9), then you must insert a floppy disk with a **System Folder** on it. The System Folder, *whether it is installed on your hard disk or stored on a floppy,* must have at least two icons in it: the System icon and the Finder icon (shown below, right). Without those two items in the machine, it can't start itself up; it will spit out any other disks you try to insert and will give you the sad-Mac face. The System Folder is an extremely important item. Although you *can* rename the folder, I strongly suggest you don't, just to keep the concept clear.

The **System** and the **Finder** are sort of like this: You are going on a trip. Your car is full of gas. You have the keys. You put a key in the ignition and start the car; the engine hums. But you can't get to where you're going yet—your car will sit in the driveway all day humming away until what? (Go ahead—think a minute.) Until you *put it in gear.* And that's sort of like what the Mac does: Your machine's plugged in. You turn it on. The screen gets

Turning It On

Internal Hard Disk

External Hard Disk

Other Switches

System Folder

System Folder

The System and The Finder

System Finder

System 7 update: System Folder, page 119. The basic concept is the same, but what you see inside the System Folder looks a little different.

bright and that little picture is flashing. But you're not going to get anywhere until you *put it in gear* by inserting a System and a Finder (the Finder runs the Desktop).

Inserting a Disk

If you *are not* working from a hard disk, then the System disk is inserted into the **internal drive** (the *drive* is the little slot in the machine that takes the disk). Disks go in with the label-side up (the side that does *not* have the *round* metal piece on it), and the metal end goes in first. Your application, or program disk, then goes into the **external drive** (usually a little box that sits on the right side of the computer). You can save data onto either disk, provided there is enough room. (Some Macs have two drive slots on the monitor; in that case, put the System disk into the top slot and the application disk into the bottom one.)

If you *are* working from a hard disk, then your applications are probably already inside the computer and you won't need to insert any other disks to access them. You'll be inserting disks to save back up copies or to install other files onto your hard disk. Either way, on the right side of the screen you will see icons, or pictures, of the start up disk and any other disks that have been inserted (see Chapter 8 for more info on icons).

Start up disk

The disk icon that appears on your Desktop in the upper right corner is the *start up* disk, the disk that holds the System Folder that booted (started) the Mac.

System and Software Versions

All computer software is constantly being upgraded and updated, making them more efficient, powerful, magical. The developers let you know which upgrade you have by labeling them with **version numbers.** At the moment of this going to press, the Macintosh System version is 6.0.7 (unless you are using System 7; see the introduction on page 5). The Finder version is 6.1.7.

As the System upgrades, the software programs are created to work with the particular nuances of the newer System, so it's a good idea to keep up on them. Although you don't *have* to use the newest System, it's usually free, so why not take advantage of it?

Only One System per Computer!

You should never have more than one System in the computer. This will invariably end in a bomb (see page 95).

CHAPTER THREE

THE DESKTOP

The **Desktop** is what you see on the screen when you first boot up your Macintosh; it's also known as the **Finder.** Consistent with the Mac environment that analogizes everything to parts of our real life, this Desktop works much the same as your desktop at home or in your office: You have desk accessories (under the Apple menu) such as a calculator, a clock, and a note pad. You have a filing cabinet (the disk) that stores all your file folders full of information. You have as many file folders as you could possibly want to organize it all. You can put folders inside of folders inside of folders *ad infinitum* (well, about 12 layers anyway) just like you would organize your hanging files. You even have a trash can.

It's a good idea to keep your Mac Desktop organized, just like you would your office desktop. Create new folders (from the File menu; also see page 33) for each category of information, and store all applicable files in it. If you create a new folder at the Desktop before you begin work in an application, then you can put your new document right into that folder when you *Save* (see page 35). This way, when you come back to the Desktop everything is organized and in its folder so nothing gets misplaced.

Whenever you Quit working in an application, Mac automatically takes you back to the Desktop. If you don't see the name "Special" in the menu, or if there is no trash can, *you are not at the Desktop*—you are still in the application. To get to your Desktop, from the File menu choose "Quit," not "Close."

The Desktop or Finder

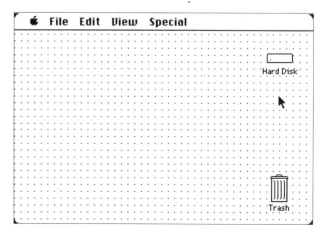

The Desktop; also known as the Finder.

Organizing Your Desktop

Below is an example of a **neatly organized Desktop window,** utilizing the *hierarchical filing system* (HFS), which is a fancy way of saying folders-inside-of-folders. Each category of software or documentation has its own place, and inside these folders may be other folders, each compartmentalizing specific data. It's much easier to keep things organized on a Macintosh Desktop than it is on an oak desktop.

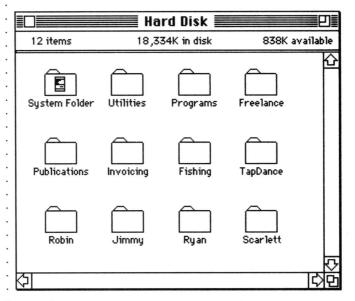

A hard disk window on the Desktop, using the folders to organize all the files.

CHAPTER FOUR

THE MOUSE

The **mouse,** of course, is that handy little piece of hardware that controls the movement of the cursor on the screen. As you move the mouse across the desk, the cursor moves across the screen in the same direction. In most Macintosh applications, you cannot fully utilize the program without the mouse. A few programs give you the option of doing absolutely everything from the keyboard if you choose; but why learn 450 keyboard commands—isn't that exactly what we're trying to avoid?

The mouse is used in several different ways:

A **single click** is a quick, light touch on the button of the mouse, with the cursor (be it a pointer or an I-beam [page 41] or anything else) located at the spot of your choice on the screen.

> A single click with the arrow on an icon at your Desktop will *select* the icon; a single click with the I-beam will *set down an insertion point.*

A **double click** is a quick click-click on the button, again with the cursor located at the appropriate spot on the screen. A double click has to be quick and the mouse must be still, or it will be interpreted as two single clicks.

> Double-clicking on a file will usually *open* that file; double-clicking on a word will *select* that word for editing.

A **press** is simply pointing to something and *holding* the mouse button down.

> Pressing with the pointer on the *menu* lets you see the commands under that item; pressing on the arrows in a scroll bar *scrolls* through that window.

Press-and-drag is to point to the object or the area of your choice, *hold/press the mouse button down,* and *drag* across, letting go when you reach your goal.

> *Choosing menu commands* is a press-and-drag function; *dragging icons* across the screen is a press-and-drag function; *selecting text* is a press-and-drag function.

The Mouse

Single Click

Double Click

Press

Press-and-Drag
(also known, misleadingly, as click-and-drag)

The Pointer When you're using the **pointer,** remember that the part of the pointer that does the trick is the *very* tip, called the "hot spot." So be sure that the extreme point is in the area you want to affect.

The hot spot . . . .

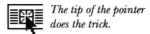

The tip of the pointer does the trick.

Cleaning the Mouse It's important and easy to **keep your mouse clean.** As you're rolling it around you can feel if any cat hairs or dustballs have gotten inside. Take it apart regularly and clean it, following these steps:

1. Take the mouse in your hand and turn it upside-down.

2. With your thumbs, slide the round wheel to the left until the little marker on the wheel points straight up to the "O" (those little symbols on the back of the mouse actually are an "O" and an "L" for Open and Lock). This will open the lid.

3. Turn it back over into your left hand so the lid and the ball fall out into your palm.

4. You can clean the ball with a soft, dry cloth; clean the rollers inside with a cotton swab dipped in rubbing alcohol.

5. When clean, put the ball in your left hand; with your right hand place the mouse on top of the ball and flop your hands over. This places the ball safely into its little cubby.

6. Put the lid back on and twist it to the right, lining up the marker with the "L" for Lock.

7. That's it!

CHAPTER FIVE

MENUS

Across the top of the screen is the **menu.** This is called a **pull-down menu,** because when you point to a menu item and *press* the mouse button down, a list of menu commands drops down.

Pull-Down Menus

🍎 File Edit View Special

The Desktop Menu

To **choose** an item in the menu, simply keep the mouse button pressed and slide the pointer down; you'll notice that certain commands become highlighted, or *selected,* as you pass over them. When the command you want is highlighted, *just **let go** of the mouse button—don't click!*

Choosing a Menu Item

In some programs the pull-down menu itself contains a **pop-out menu** where you not only slide *down*, but also *out to the side,* usually in the direction of the arrow.

Pop-Out Menus

In the list, you can see that some **commands** are in **black** letters and some commands are in **gray.** When a command is gray, it means that particular item is not available at that moment.

The most common reason that a command is unavailable is that something was not *selected* before you went to the menu. For instance, you cannot choose "Open" from the File menu if you haven't first selected a disk or file as the item to be opened (to select something, click *once* on it).

Gray vs. Black Commands

Keyboard Command Shortcuts

File	
New Folder	⌘N
Open	⌘O
Get Info	⌘I
Eject	⌘E

To the right of the commands in the pull-down menu you often see a little code, such as ⌘ N. This is a keyboard shortcut you can use *instead* of using the menu. If you hold down the Command key (the one with the cloverleaf symbol on it: ⌘) and press the letter associated with it, then the computer reacts just as if you had chosen that command from the menu. For instance, if you click once on a file to select it and then press ⌘ O, the selected file will open just as if you had chosen that command from the File menu with the mouse.

The people who designed the Mac interface have been very thoughtful—as many as possible of the keyboard shortcuts are alliterative: ⌘O **O**pens files; ⌘ P **P**rints; ⌘ E **E**jects; ⌘ W closes **W**indows; etc. Also see the following chapter.

Ellipses... & Dialog Boxes

Anytime you see an ellipsis (the three dots: **...**) after a menu command (as in "Open..."), it means you will get a dialog box. There are different varieties of dialog boxes, such as alert boxes or message boxes, but basically they all are meant to communicate with you.

Dialog boxes always give you an option to Cancel, so it is quite safe to go exploring menu commands this way. Just choose a command that is followed by an ellipsis, check out the dialog box, then click Cancel. Even if you clicked around on buttons or typed in the dialog box, clicking Cancel will make sure none of your changes are put into effect.

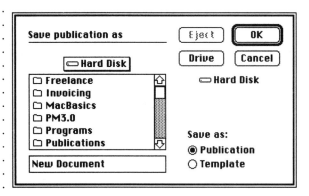

 A "Save as..." dialog box; notice you can Cancel.
You can also choose to eject a floppy disk before you Cancel if you need to eject or swap disks.

CHAPTER SIX

IMPORTANT KEYS

There are several keys on the Macintosh **keyboard** that are particularly important and useful. They come in handy for shortcuts, manipulating images, accessing alternate characters, and any number of things in specific applications.

Speaking of keyboards, there are basically three kinds for the Mac: two *standard* keyboards with the keypad at the end (like a ten-key adding machine)—one version for the Mac Plus and older models, and one for SEs, Classics, and similar models—and the *extended* keyboard that has all the function keys and other little arcane sets of keys. Often people think the *standard* keyboard is the *extended* one because it has the numeric keypad that we didn't have on our typewriters. It isn't. All the keyboards generally have standard characters, but there are several keys that are placed differently, depending on which model you have. No matter where they are placed, though, all keyboards have the following keys, and they all operate the same.

The symbols noted under each heading are the symbols that appear in menus to indicate pressing that key. They are usually used in combination with letters—always hold down all the descriptor keys (Command, Shift, etc.) and give a quick tap on the let·er key associated with it. For instance, to Open files the command is often ⌘ **O**: hold down the Command key while typing a quick O.

The **Command key** is on the bottom row, the key with the California freeway cloverleaf symbol on it: ⌘. On the SE and extended keyboards it also has an apple on it, and you may hear it referred to as the "Apple key." The symbols you see in the menu are referring to this key, and most applications have keyboard shortcuts using it.

Next to the Command Key is the **Option key.** It's often used in combination with the Command key and/or the Shift key. It's through the Option key that you access the special characters, such as ¢ and ®, as well as accent marks, as in résumé and piñata (see page 48–50).

The **Backspace key,** called **Delete** on most keyboards, is located on the upper right. The name was changed to

The Keyboard

Command Key
⌘

Option Key

Backspace *or* Delete Key

Delete because that's really what it does—whatever is *selected* will be removed when the Delete key is hit; whatever letter is to the *left* of the insertion point will be deleted as it is backspaced over.

Tilde Key
~
The Tilde key (~) is located on the upper left of some keyboards and next to the Spacebar on others, including the extended keyboards. It's often called the Undo Key,

Escape Key
esc
because in certain applications it will undo the action immediately preceding. Although on the SE and the extended keyboards the upper left key now says **esc** (*escape*) and the Tilde has been placed next to the Spacebar, in many applications *esc* can still be considered the Undo key because it often does the same thing.

Control Key
The Control key, found only on the bigger keyboards, doesn't do much yet; in most applications it's just a dead key. They say it's something we'll grow into. You *can* type the Command key symbol with it: in the Chicago font, press Control Q to produce ⌘ (*but not in System 7*).

Return Key
The Return key is often used for other procedures than simply starting a new paragraph. For instance, any button in any dialog box that has the double border around it can be activated with the Return key instead of the mouse. Different programs use it in different ways.

Enter Key
⌄
The Enter key on the keypad will also activate buttons with the double border, just the same as the Return key as noted above. Again, different programs use the Enter key in different ways.

Spacebar
⎵
The Spacebar is represented in menus by the symbol shown to the left *or as a blank space*. That'll really throw you. How long does it take to figure out that ⇧⌘ means press the Shift key, the Command key, and the Spacebar?

Shift Key
⇧
The Shift key is one of the most common keys used in keyboard shortcuts, symbolized by an upward arrow.

Caps Lock

Just a note: the Caps Lock key does *not* act just like the Shift Lock on a typewriter—in Caps Lock you get capital letters, yes, but you do *not* get the characters above the numbers or above the punctuation. If you want the Shift-characters you must still press the Shift key to get them. Some keyboard shortcuts will not work if the Caps Lock key is down, so check for that if you're having problems.

CHAPTER SEVEN

WINDOWS

A **window,** as shown below, is a basic, fundamental interface of the Macintosh. If you imagine your disk as a filing cabinet in which you store all your work in manila folders, then opening windows is like opening file drawers to see what's in the cabinet. It's important to know all the little tricks in using a window, as you'll find windows in almost every application. They're simple and fun to control.

Windows

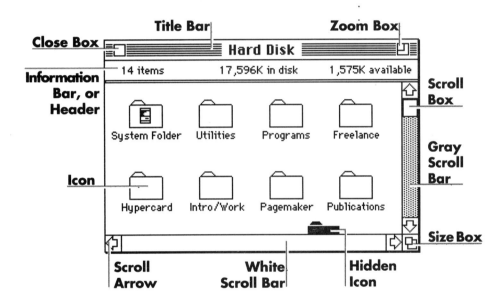

The **title bar** is the area at the top of the window in which, logically, the title appears. This title refers to the disk, folder, or document you have opened. If you press-and-drag in the title bar, you can **move** the window around the Desktop; it moves as an outline. Just let go when you have the outline placed where you want.

Title Bar

Moving the Window

If you have more than one window open, only one will have lines in its title bar; this means it's the **window.** If the windows are overlapping, the active window is the one that is foremost.

Active Window

The active window is the window that the commands from the keyboard or the menu will affect. For instance,

System 7 update: Windows, page 109; menu in title bar, page 111.

if you go to the File menu and chose "Close," it will close the active window. If you ask for a "New Folder," the new folder will appear in the active window.

To Make the Window Active

To make a window **active,** simply click on any visible part of it; this will also bring that window to the front of any others. You may have to move other windows around in order to see the window you want to make active.

> To move a window *without* making it active, hold down the Command key while you press-and-drag in its title bar.

Gray Icons

Sometimes you can't see the window itself but you *can* see its **gray icon;** in that case, double-click on the gray icon to bring its window forward and thus make it active. (Also see pages 29 and 98 regarding gray icons.)

Size Box

On the bottom right corner is the **size box.** If you press-and-drag in the size box, you will make the window larger or smaller.

Zoom Box

On the upper right corner is the **zoom box.** If you click in the zoom box it will enlarge to fill almost the entire Desktop. If you click in it when it's large, the window will zoom back down to the size it was *just before* you zoomed it larger.

Scroll Bars

Along the right and bottom edges of the window are the **scroll bars.** The scroll bars allow you to view everything in the window, even if it cannot all fit on the Desktop or if the window is sized too small. You'll notice in the example on page 21 that the scroll bar along the right side is gray, while the one on the bottom is white.

Gray Scroll Bar

When a **scroll bar is gray,** it's indicating that there are other items in the window you can't see. In the example on the previous page, you can see a folder along the bottom edge that is barely visible, so the scroll bar is gray, telling you something more is beyond its borders.

White Scroll Bar

When the **scroll bar is white,** it's indicating there is nothing more in the direction of the arrows (the horizontal direction in the diagram) than what you can see.

Scroll Arrows

At either end of the scroll bars are the **scroll arrows.** When the scroll bar is *gray* you can press on a scroll arrow, making the contents of the window glide past you as the scenery outside a train window.

System 7 update: active window and zoom box, page 110

Notice the little **scroll box** in each scroll bar. As you press on the arrows, this box moves so you can see where you are in the window. When the box is all the way at one end, that's the end of the window.

Another useful technique using the scroll box is this: if you press-and-drag the scroll box, you can move it to any position on the scroll bar, let go, and the window will immediately jump to that particular place rather than scrolling through everything. This is very handy inside an application where you have a long document and scrolling with the arrows would take too long. In some applications a number appears within the scroll box to indicate what page you're on.

There's yet another way to use the scroll bars: if you simply **click** the pointer in any *gray* area of the bar, the window will move up, down, or across, usually a full window view—what was at the bottom of the view will then be at the top or vice-versa.

Just under the title bar you'll find some very useful **information:** *if your window is showing icons,* you'll see how many items are in that window, how much space is being used up on the disk, and how much space is left on the disk. On a hard disk, the numbers are still referring to kilobytes, so just round it off to megs by referring to the number in the thousands place (e.g., 7,856K would be almost 8 megs). *If your window is not showing icons,* then the information bar indicates how your files are currently being organized (see "Viewing the Window," below).

And, of course, in the upper left is the **close box.** Clicking once in that little box will close the window for you, sending it back to the disk or folder it came from.

The Macintosh always tries to allow things to happen in a way that you feel is most workable for *you.* The **view of the window** is another good example—you can choose to see what's in your window in a variety of ways, all appropriate for different purposes or styles.

These different views are found, of course, in the View menu when you're at your Desktop. When you choose one, the active window will appear in that choice (the active window, remember, is the one that has the lines in its title bar). The view will stay that way until you

Scroll Box

Scroll Box

Clicking in the Scroll Bar

Information Bar, or Header

| 4 items | 596K in disk | 175K available |

Close Box

Viewing the Window

System 7 update: Scrolling, page 110; Info bar, or header, page 123; major conveniences in viewing and customizing the window, page 110.

Name
☐ Children
☐ Freelance
☐ HC Book
☐ Hypercard
☐ Intro/Works
☐ Tap Dance
☐ Utilities

Notice the underline in the information bar indicating which view is being displayed.

change it. As you change the views, you'll notice the name of the view you have chosen is underlined in the window.

While viewing the files as a list, you can still manipulate them just as if they were icons (i.e., pick them up and put them in the trash or in another folder, rename them, copy them, open them, etc.; see Chapter 8 on Icons).

View by Small Icon keeps that feeling of looking at pictures, if that's what you prefer, but the icons are tiny so you can fit more in the window. They're not in any specific order.

View by Icon is what you typically see—pictures representing the data. Visually-oriented people tend to prefer this style. Again, the files are in no specific order.

View by Name turns the icons into text for those who prefer looking at words rather than pictures. A tiny little icon is still present so you can see what sort of file it is. They're listed in alphabetical order by name.

View by Date lists the files in chronological order backwards from the date they were last *modified,* not the date they were originally created. This is handy when you have, for instance, several budget documents and you want to see the most recent version.

View by Size lists the files in order of size, beginning with the largest. It tells you how many K (kilobytes) that particular file is taking up on your disk. This is handy if you need to remove something to make room; you can see which files to remove to clear enough space. Unfortunately, it won't show the size of folders; to find their size you need to select the folder and choose "Get Info" from the File menu (see page 31).

View by Kind lists the files in groups of applications, documents, or folders. This is handy if you want to see a list of all your applications, or all the documents in your budget folder, etc.

View by Kind is particularly useful for a folder that holds an application and all its accessories—dictionaries, tutorials, technical files, samples, etc. This view will always put the application itself at the *top* of the list so it's easy to find.

When you're viewing *icons* in your window, they often get all scrumbled up and look like a mess. To align them all nicely, simply choose **Clean Up Window** from the Special menu—all the icons will fly to the nearest little cubby available on the underlying invisible grid.

> When they fly to the nearest spot on the grid, though, there are often spaces left available where another icon could fit in. If you want them to all line up in rows, from left to right with no empty places, hold down the Option key when you choose "Clean Up Window."

If an icon is *selected,* then the menu will say "Clean Up Selection," in which case just that selected item will be straightened up. Older systems may just say, "Clean Up." It works the same.

This is the button I want in my house—the dishes jump onto their shelves, the laundry puts itself away in the drawers, and all the toys go back in the toybox.

To **close** all the windows that are open on your Desktop, hold down the Option key while clicking the active window's close box; they'll all go away one after another!

> If you have System 6.0 or higher, you'll notice in the File menu there is a keyboard command for closing the active window: Command W. If you want to close all the windows at once, press Command Option W and *all* the windows will fly away home.
>
> *Note: Unless you are in System 7, this will not work if a Desk Accessory is the* active *window; nor will it work if the Caps Lock key is down.*

> Another fancy trick to close all the windows is to hold down the Option key when you choose "Quit" from any application. *Keep holding the Option key down until you see your Desktop.* When you arrive, there won't be a single window open. If you use this trick you can legitimately call yourself a Power User.

> Often the file you want to open is buried within several folders. Hold the Option key down while you double-click to open those folders. They'll close up behind you as you go along.

Clean Up Window

Close All the Windows

Print the Window on an ImageWriter

Occasionally you may have a need to **print** the information you find in a particular **window;** for instance, to make a list of all the documents that are on that floppy disk, or all the dated budget files that are in the Budget folder. *You can't do this on a laser printer, though.*

To print the info in the window:

▼ Turn on your printer.

▼ Make sure the window that contains the data you want is the active window (click once on it).

▼ Hold down the Command and Shift keys and press 4 (**Command Shift 4**); when the printer responds you can let go.

Print the Screen

The above procedure prints only the *visible* contents of the *active window;* if you want to **print everything on the screen,** the whole screen and nothing but the screen, then do the same as above but this time press the **Caps Lock** down before you press **Command Shift 4.** This way you can print the contents of any and all open windows.

If you want to print a picture of your screen on your laser printer (and you are not using System 7), you can create and print a screen dump, or screen shot. See page 30.

System 7 update: print the window or the screen to a laser printer, page 107.

CHAPTER EIGHT

ICONS

Icons

Icons—the little pictures you see on the screen—are another intrinsic part of the Mac interface. Instead of having to type in a code to get into an application or document, you simply click on the icon representing it.

> A note about clicking on icons—if you're trying to select or open it, don't click on the *name,* or the icon thinks you want to change the name.

Disk Icons

Floppy disk

Hard disk

When you initially turn on your machine and get to the Desktop (as on page 13), you'll always see an icon of the **disk** you're using, whether it's a hard disk or a floppy (the hard disk icon may look different than this one shown, depending on where it is and what kind it is).

▾ Single-clicking on a disk icon will select it.

▾ Double-clicking on a disk icon will open it to show you a window holding all the files.

> *Note:* If a disk icon is gray, it is either already open (page 29) or has been left in RAM after being ejected (page 98).

Folder Icons

Whenever you have a window open, most likely you'll see **folder icons.** They act just like folders in your filing cabinet. Be sure to read the following chapter on Folders, as they are an important organizational tool.

▾ Single-clicking on a folder will select it.

▾ Double-clicking will open it to show you a window with all the files that are stored in that folder.

System Icons

Inside the folder named System Folder are all the **system icons** that help run the Macintosh, as well as a variety of icons that are for extra or fancy options. The ones that look like little Macs are system icons that perform essential operations. You'll see one called System and one called Finder—if those two are not inside the System Folder, you won't even be able to use your machine.

▾ Single-clicking on a system icon will select it.

▾ Double-clicking will give you a message telling you an application can't be found or that it is locked or in use. That's because system icons are just visual

System 7 update: renaming and creating your own icons, page 112; folder icons, page 109; system icons, page 119.

representations of the data on your disk that makes them work—there's really nothing to look at besides the cute little icon.

Printer Icons

Also in your System Folder are **printer icons.** In order to print to any printer, you must first have the icon inside your System Folder. If it is not in the System Folder, then when you go to the Chooser (see page 81) to tell Mac which printer you want to use, there will be nothing to designate and you won't be able to print.

  ▾ Single-clicking on a printer icon will select it.
  ▾ Double-clicking will give you the same message as the one you get with the system icons, for the same reason.

Application or Program Icons

MacPaint

MacWrite II

The **application (or program) icons** are the fancy ones. These belong to the actual applications (the software programs). Each application has its own design, so they all look different, but what they have in common is that they all try to give some sort of visual clue as to what they do. For instance, in the icons to the left you can see that MacPaint is an art program; MacWrite II is a word processing program.

  ▾ Single-clicking on an application icon will select it.
  ▾ Double-clicking will either open to a new, blank page within that program, or at least to a dialog box where you can choose to *create* a new, blank page.

Document Icons

Peaches

Article

Document icons represent documents, or files, that you have created in any particular application. Whenever you are working in an application and you save your document with a title, a document icon is created for you on your Desktop.

Document icons almost always look like a piece of paper with the top right corner folded down, or perhaps a sheaf of papers or a stack of cards. Typically they have some resemblance to the application they were created in, as you can see by the MacPaint and the MacWrite icons on the left.

  ▾ Single-clicking on a document icon will select it.
  ▾ Double-clicking will usually open the application in which the document was created, with that particular document on the screen. (If you get an error message, check page 94, "Can't open a file.")

When an **icon is gray,** as the one on the right, that means it's *already open*. Maybe you don't see the icon's window because it's hidden behind another open window, but you know it's open somewhere. (If a floppy disk icon is gray, but it is not in the machine, see page 98!)

▾ Single-clicking on an open icon will select it.

▾ Double-clicking will bring its window to the front as the active window.

When an **icon is black,** like the one on the right, that means it is *selected*—it got selected by someone clicking once on it. Once an icon is selected, you can press-and-drag it somewhere; menu commands will affect it, such as Open or Put Away or Clean Up Selection; you can change its name by typing.

Highlighted (Black) Icons

Scarlett

▾ Single-clicking is what selected this icon in the first place.

▾ Double-clicking a selected icon will open it just like any other icon.

The **trash can icon** works just like the trash can in your yard—you put things in it you don't want anymore and the garbage collector comes and takes it away and you never see it again.

Trash Can Icon

To put something in the trash: Press-and-drag an icon over to it. *When the can becomes black,* let go and the icon will drop inside. If you find a bunch of garbage hanging around outside the can, it's because you didn't wait for the can to turn black—you just set it down next to it. Try again. The *tip of the pointer* must touch the can!

To remove something from the trash: If you double-click on the trash can you'll find that it opens up to a window, just like any other window. So if you decide you want that item you just threw away, you can go get it. Either press-and-drag the icon back to the disk/folder it came from; **or** click once on it to select it, then from the File menu choose "Put Away" and it will go right back where it came from. How does it know?

Don't count on anything staying in the trash very long, though! Read on . . .

System 7 update: Trash can, page 103.

You can empty the trash by going up to the Special menu and requesting "Empty Trash." Once you do that, it's gone forever. No amount of crying or pleading or screaming or kicking will bring it back. Believe me.

Now, you can empty the trash yourself, as noted above. But sometimes the garbage collector comes when you're not looking, so don't count on it staying there 'til you empty it. Whenever you eject a disk, copy a file, Shut Down, Restart, or turn off the computer, the trash gets emptied. Whenever you open an application, the trash gets emptied. Whenever the power goes out, even for a split second, the trash gets emptied. And if the Mac runs out of RAM (Random Aaccess Memory, where everything stays until it gets saved to a disk), Mac herself will empty the trash for you and take that memory space. So be careful.

Whenever anything Mac thinks is important has been put in the trash, such as an application or system icon, you'll get a dialog box asking if you really want to throw that away. That's nice.

If you don't want to see the warning dialog box, hold down the Option key while trashing the item.

Unfortunately, Mac doesn't think anything *you* have created is worth warning you about.

When trashing items to make more space on the disk, the trash must be emptied before the space will open up; watch the numbers in the information bar of the window when you empty the trash.

Screen Dump

Screen 0

Occasionally you will see or create an icon that is named Screen 0 or Screen 1, etc.; this is a **screen dump.** A screen dump is a picture of the computer screen at the time you pressed the special key combination.

Whenever you press Command Shift 3, a MacPaint screen dump, or screen shot, is created for you; an icon for the shot will appear in the window that contains the System Folder. You can open MacPaint, open this file (or use almost any paint program with the MacPaint button in the Open box chosen), and view/change the image just like you would any other paint image. Then paste it into another document.

For instance, all the images in this book were created using screen shots. With the image on the screen in its natural habitat, I pressed Command Shift 3. Then I opened DeskPaint and opened the Screen 0 file that had been created. Since the screen shot took a picture of the entire screen, I had to erase all the excess stuff around the image. Then I could change, resize, rotate, flop, etc., the graphic. I put the images in the Scrapbook (page 86) and later pasted them onto these pages.

You can create up to 10 screen dumps, and they'll be labeled 0 to 9. You can create more, but you have to rename the others first.

Get Info is not an icon, but a menu item that can give you important information about any file represented by an icon on your Desktop, be it application, document, system, printer, or folder.

Select an icon, any icon, by clicking once on it; then from the File menu choose "Get Info." You'll get a little information window that tells you interesting things about the file, such as how big it is, when it was made, which software program it was created in, which software version you have.

The nicest thing about this window is you can type in your own information in the box at the bottom (the insertion point flashes, waiting for you to type). This comes in very handy: you can write notes to yourself about that particular file and what it contains, briefly detail this budget file from that budget file, record any bugs you find in it, make note of further changes you want to employ, leave notes for your lover, etc. The information you type is automatically saved. (If at some point you chooose to rebuild your Desktop [see page 92], the rebuilding process will unfortunately destroy any Get Info notes. Darn it.) *(Even happens in System 7.)*

The info on the following page explains the little "Locked" checkbox you see in the upper right.

Get Info

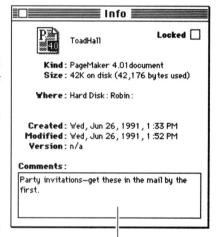

This is the box in which you can type your own notes.

Locking the File

Locked ☒
This file is now locked.

There is a **Locked** checkbox in the upper right corner of the Get Info window. If you check this box (click once on it), the file cannot be renamed or inadvertently thrown away—as soon as it hits the trash a dialog box will come up telling you a locked file cannot be thrown away.

It also becomes a *Read-Only* file: anyone can open and read the file, but no one can save any changes to it. This is handy for sending around copies of a document and ensuring no one accidentally changes anything. You can't even change the Get Info notes.

> If you hold down the Option key, you *can* throw away a locked file. Uh oh.

Locked ☐
This file is now unlocked.

To unlock the file, simply click in the checkbox again. If there is no X, it is unlocked.

Moving Icons

To **move icons,** simply press-and-drag on them. You can put any icon into or drag any icon out of any folder icon. Also see Chapter 10 on Copying/Selecting.

Renaming Icons

To **rename an icon,** click once on it. When it turns black, simply type and the name will change. If the name does not change, click once more on the icon; sometimes it insists on *two single clicks (not a double-click!)* as a safety feature protecting you from changing the name accidentally. Use standard word processing procedures to set an insertion point, double-click a *word* to select it, backspace to delete, etc., as detailed in Chapter 12 on Typing.

Undo Icon Name Change

If you perchance do accidentally change the name of an icon (which is very easy to do—files have been known to mysteriously change their names to \\\\\\\\\\\\\ or `````` while you weren't doing anything but leaning on the keyboard), you do have one chance to restore it to its original form: Undo. As soon as you see this mistake has been made, from the File menu choose "Undo." *If you haven't done anything* since this minor catastophe (and things could be worse), Undo will restore the original name, even if you forgot it. If you are too late to catch Undo, you'll just have to rename it yourself.

System 7 update: renaming icons, page 112.

CHAPTER NINE

FOLDERS

Folders

Folders are essential to the organization of your work on the Mac. They are, of course, visual representations of our office and home environment, and they function in much the same way.

You can consider your disk to be the main filing cabinet. When you store items in a filing cabinet, you don't just toss them in the drawer, do you? Can you imagine what a mess your filing cabinet would be without folders? Many Macintoshes become just as messy and just as difficult to find work in. It's very important to learn to take advantage of the folders.

Creating a New Folder

You can **create your own** new, empty folders by choosing "New Folder" from the File menu, or by using the keyboard shortcut, Command N. The new folder will appear in the *active* window.

Naming the New Folder

The new folder shows up in the active window already highlighted, or selected (it's black), with the name "Empty Folder." Mac assumes you want to change the name, so while it is black you can just type the name you want it to have and the new name will appear. If you type an error, just backspace over it (use the Backspace or Delete key in the upper right of the keyboard) and continue typing. You can use up to 27 characters, but you can't use a colon.

Changing the Name of a Folder

If you accidently unhighlighted the new folder before you changed its name, or if you want to change the name of any other folder, it is still very easy to do: simply click on the folder and it will turn black. You'll notice the pointer changes from an arrow to an I-beam when it's pointing to the *name* of the folder; this is a visual clue that whatever you type now will replace the title that is already there. So go ahead and type the new name while the folder's black.

The pointer changes to an I-beam.

If typing while the folder is highlighted doesn't change its name, click once more on the folder; sometimes it insists on *two single clicks (not a double-click!)* as a safety feature protecting you from changing the name accidentally.

System 7 update: expanding and compressing folders, page 109; creating a new folder, page 111; renaming icons, page 112.

**Putting
Something
Inside a Folder**

To put something **inside** the folder, press-and-drag any icon over to it; when the folder turns black, let go and the icon will pop inside. The folder does not have to be open to place an item inside of it, and it can be gray. You can have folders inside of folders inside of folders, which is technically called the *Hierarchical File System* (HFS).

**Opening
a Folder**

Double-clicking on any folder will **open** it to a window, showing you all the valuable information you have stored inside.

**Removing
Something
From a Folder**

To **remove** something, open the folder first, so you see its window and the icons inside, as below. Then simply press-and-drag the icon(s) out, either to the Desktop or to another folder or window.

**Note:
Moving as
opposed to Copying**

If you are moving the icon to someplace else on the *same* disk, it will just pop out of that one folder and into the other. BUT if you are moving the item to a *different* disk, the original icon will stay put and a *copy* of it will be placed on the other disk. (See the tips on pages 37–38.)

**Organizing
Your Disk
Using Folders**

Below is an example of a well-organized hard disk; there isn't a bunch of junk lying around making it difficult to find things. *(Would that houses were so easy to keep neat!)* It's basically organized the same way a filing cabinet would be.

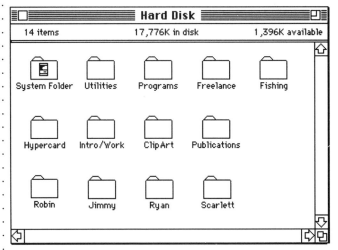

*Everything on the disk (the "filing cabinet") is tucked into a folder.
The folders may each have sub-folders to further organize their contents.*

System 7 update: expanding and compressing folders, pages 109.

One of the best ways to keep windows tidy is to **create a specific new folder** for a new project *before* you create the documents for the project, and then *save the documents right into their own folder.* For instance, if you are about to create a budget report with seven variations, or a newsletter in which there will be ten to twelve separate stories, then follow these steps:

Creating Project-Specific Folders ▽

> **At your Desktop,** *before* **you open the application** to start creating the reports, make your new folder and name it (let's name this one *Budget News*). This new folder can be inside of another folder, of course.

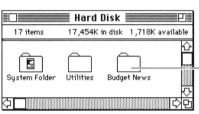

The new folder in the hard disk window, waiting for new stories to be stored inside.

▼ Open your application and create the first report.

▼ When you go to "Save As…" and name the story, find the folder *Budget News* in the Save As dialog box. In the list box you'll see the name of the folder you created earlier. Double-click the name to open the folder.

In this example, here is the folder Budget News; double-click on it to open it.

If you don't see the folder listed here, perhaps you have it tucked inside of another folder, in which case you will need to open that other folder first. Or click Drive to see if it is on another disk.

▾ After you double-click on the name of the folder, you will see its name and an open folder icon in the label above the list box, as shown below. If you choose to Save right now, it will be saved into *that* folder.

*Make sure this **title** shows the name of your folder. If you see the name of your folder in the list box beneath it, double-click on that name to open the folder and make its name appear here.*

Whenever you save a file, it is always saved into whatever folder or onto whatever disk appears in this title.

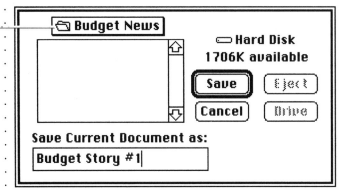

▾ When you go back to your Desktop everything will be right where it belongs, tucked into its own folder, and nothing will be forgotten or misplaced.

If you refuse to read and follow these directions and have lost files, do read about Mr. Find File on page 83. He'll find them for you.

CHAPTER TEN

COPYING/ SELECTING

Copying files is an everyday task. You may need to copy an application from its original disk onto your hard disk; copy a report to give to a co-worker; copy a document to take to a service bureau for printing; create the ever-necessary backup copy; etc. etc. etc.

Why Copy?

Apple has made it as easy as can possibly be to **copy** files on the Mac (which is why *pirating,* or copying software without paying for it, is such a problem for software developers).

Copying

> **To copy,** simply click on the icon representing the file you want to copy; then press-and-drag the icon to the icon of the disk you want to copy it onto. A little message comes up telling you it's being copied. That's it.

You may copy onto a disk, into a folder on another disk, or onto your hard drive. In every case, make sure that the icon of the place you are copying *into* turns *black.* When the icon is black, that means it's ready to accept the file/s. If the icon is not black, you'll just be placing it *next* to the icon, not *inside* of it. The *tip of the pointer* is what turns any icon black.

Actually, the *copying* process only takes place if you drag the file to another *disk.* If you want to make a copy of the file on the *same* disk, click *once* on the file icon, then from the File menu choose "Duplicate" (or press Command D). This creates a second version in the same folder named "Copy of ____." When you duplicate or copy folders, every item contained within that folder is also copied.

Duplicate/Copy File on Same Disk

> If you want to put a *copy of a file into another folder on the same disk,* hold down the Option key while moving the file. (This does not rename the file "Copy of ____.")

To **copy more than one** file at a time, *select* more than one file (detailed in the next paragraph). When more than one file is selected, dragging one file will drag them all together, either to the trash can, into another folder, onto another disk, or simply to clean up the joint.

Copying More Than One File at a Time

Selecting More Than One File at a Time

You may have noticed in a Desktop window that when you *press in an empty space and drag the pointer,* a dotted rectangle comes out of the tip—this is the **selection marquee,** common in many Mac programs. On the Desktop, any file·that is even partially enclosed in this marquee will be selected.

The selection marquee—just press-and-drag with the pointer tool.

Selecting all the icons this way will of course turn them all black.

▼ When you press-and-drag on the *black* area of one of the selected items, they will all drag together.

▼ Clicking in any *white* space will *deselect* all the files.

Shift-Clicking to Select More Than One File

Another method of selecting more than one item is to **Shift-click.** You may have noticed that once a file is selected, clicking on another file deselects the first one. *But,* if you hold down the Shift key while clicking, every one of the files you click will be selected. This way you can select several files in different corners of your window.

Shift-Clicking to Deselect

In the same manner, you can **deselect** one file at a time. For instance, if you group a bunch of files within the selection marquee but you don't want the one in the middle, simply hold down the Shift key and click once on that one—it will be the only one deselected.

Copy From Floppy to Floppy with Only One Floppy Drive

If you want to know how to copy from one floppy disk to another floppy disk when you have only one floppy drive, please see page 91x.

System 7 update: cool selection tips, page 110.

CHAPTER ELEVEN

OPENING APPLICATIONS
Or Documents

The term **application** is often used synonomously with **program.** It refers to the software package you are using to create your documents, such as Claris MacPaint, Microsoft Works, Adobe Illustrator, etc. They all do something different; they all have a particular function. Sometimes it takes a little research to find the software applications to meet your specific needs.

To open an **application,** or software program, find its icon on the disk. Application icons, as noted in the chapter on icons, typically look fancier than anything else. Whether the program is installed on your hard disk or you are using a floppy disk, you will need to find its icon at the Desktop.

> From the Desktop, double-click on the application icon to open to a blank page, ready for you to create a new document.

> Some applications open to a commercial, or at least to an Open dialog box; in either case you can choose to create a new document at that point from the File menu.

To **open a document** that has already been created and saved in an application, find its icon on your Desktop.

> Double-click on a document icon; most of the time this will open the application, placing your document on the screen as you last saved it.

A few programs won't allow you to open their documents from the Desktop. If the software program itself is *in* the computer, either on the hard disk or on a floppy, and you get the dialog box telling you an application can't be found, then you must *open the application first* and *then* open the document from the File menu by choosing "Open." See the section on the following page for tips on maneuvering around the Open dialog box.

Now, just because you have an icon representing a document you created in a certain software application doesn't mean you can open up that document just anywhere. Double-clicking on a document icon will only

What is an Application?

Opening an Application

MacPaint

Application icon

Opening a Document from the Desktop

Peaches

Document icon

Important Note!

open it **IF** *the application itself is also in the computer,* either on the hard disk or on a floppy disk that is inserted into one of the drives. If the application isn't there, then the document doesn't have anywhere to put itself! (See page 94, "Can't Open a File," for more info.)

New vs. Open

Once the application is up and running, in the File menu you see two choices: **New** and **Open.** This confused me at first because I thought, "Well, I want to *open* a *new* one." The difference is this:

- ▼ **New** creates a clean, blank page on which you can begin a *new* document.

- ▼ **Open** takes you to a dialog box (shown below) where you can choose to *open* a document that has been previously created and saved.

An "Open" Dialog Box

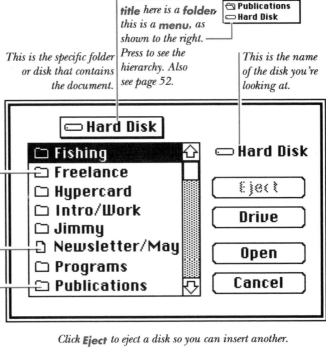

When the icon in the title here is a folder, this is a menu, as shown to the right. Press to see the hierarchy. Also see page 52.

This is the specific folder or disk that contains the document.

This is the name of the disk you're looking at.

Folder names are black (not gray) because there may be a file inside that you can open.

Single-click on one of these names to select that file.

Double-click the name to open the file.

If the icon is a folder, as this one is, it will open here in this list box to show you the files inside the folder; if the icon is a document, it will open that document on your screen.

MacBooks
Publications
Hard Disk

Hard Disk

Fishing
Freelance
Hypercard
Intro/Work
Jimmy
Newsletter/May
Programs
Publications

Hard Disk

Eject

Drive

Open

Cancel

Click **Eject** *to eject a disk so you can insert another.*

Click **Drive** *to see what's on the disk in the other drive.*

Click **Open** *to open the selected file;* **or** *you can double-click on the file name.*

Click **Cancel** *to take you back to wherever you were without opening anything.*

CHAPTER TWELVE

TYPING

In some applications **typing** is the main idea, as in a word processor. In some, it is the way to input the data whose purpose is to be manipulated, as in a database or a spreadsheet. In others, it is a sideline that is occasionally necessary, as in a paint program. And everywhere you find dialog boxes where you type some answer or other, and even on your Desktop you type the names of files and folders. Fortunately, in the consistent Mac environment, every program reacts to typing in the same way.

Typing

You may already be familiar with the Macintosh word processing **I-beam** (pronounced eye-beam): ⌶

The I-Beam

In the Macintosh, the I-beam is a visual clue that you are now in a typing mode, as opposed to having an arrow or a cross-hair or any number of other cursors that appear in various programs.

> *The I-beam is simply another pointer.* And just like the pointer, it doesn't do anything until you *click* it.

When you move the I-beam pointer to a spot and click, it sets down a flashing **insertion point** that looks like this: | (but it flashes).

The Insertion Point

After you click the mouse to set the insertion point, then you can move the I-beam out of the way (using the mouse)—**the *insertion point* is what you need to begin typing.** With the insertion point flashing, anything you type will start at that point and move out to the right. This is true whether the insertion point is at the beginning or the end of a paragraph, in the middle of a word, in a field of a dialog box, under an icon at your Desktop, or anywhere else. (The only time the words will not move to the right is if the alignment has been set to align right or centered, or if a tab other than left-aligned has been set.) At any time you can take the mouse, move the I-beam pointer somewhere else, click it, and start typing from the new insertion point.

Also from that insertion point, pressing the **Backspace** key (found in the upper right, appropriately renamed the **Delete** key on the newer keyboards) will backspace

Backspace/ Delete

over and remove any letters in its path. So you can backspace/delete to correct typos as you go, or set the insertion point down anywhere else in your text and backspace/delete from there.

Highlighting Text

Highlighting text is a shortcut to backspacing over letters to remove them. All through the Mac environment, if you double-click on a word with the I-beam, the entire word is selected, indicated by the highlighting.

This **word** is highlighted.

If you want to select more than one word, press-and-drag over the entire area you wish to highlight.

Part of this line is highlighted.

What does highlighting do? Well, once a word is highlighted (selected), anything you type will *entirely replace* the highlighted text. Or you can now change the font (typeface) or style or size of the text using your menu commands. Or you can copy or cut or delete that text. Or you can paste something in to replace it. In fact, you *cannot* do any of these things *unless* the text is first highlighted. (Each of these procedures is explained in this chapter.)

To **unhighlight,** click once anywhere, even in the black space.

When to Use the Return Key

Word wrap: In a word processor, you *never* want to hit the Return key at the end of your line, *unless* it is the end of the paragraph or unless you *really do* want the line to end there, as in an address. This is because word processors *word wrap*—the words just wrap themselves around onto the next line when they get to the right margin. Why is that? Well . . .

Hard return: What happens when you press the Return key is that you insert what is called a *hard return.* Then if you were to change your margins, your line would *always* break at that hard return, even if there are only two words on the line. So, just keep those nimble fingers moving along and only hit the Return key when you want a new paragraph.

Double-space: Hitting the Return key twice is like pushing the carriage return on a typewriter twice—you get a double space between the lines. This is for extra space between paragraphs (although in most word processors you can ask for an automatic increase of space between paragraphs). If you want the entire document, or even just a piece of it, double-spaced—that's different; there is always an instant way to change your spacing to double-spaced. Check your manual for the method for your particular application.

Removing a Return: The computer sees a Return as just another character, which means to remove a Return you simply *backspace over it,* just like to remove an unwanted character. The problem is, in most programs you can't *see* the Return character. So you must set the insertion point just to the left of the first character on the line and backspace/delete, like so:

|Set the insertion point at the beginning of the line (as shown here) and backspace to *remove the empty line* above this one. Backspace/delete *again* to *wrap the sentence back up* to the one above.

The computer deals with **blank spaces** just as it deals with the characters you can see. Every tab, return, spacebar space, etc., is a character to Mac. This means you can select blank spaces, blank lines, blank tabbed spaces, or Returns in order to delete them. Select and delete them just like you would any other character.

Blank Spaces

The space between
these ▮▮▮▮▮▮words is highlighted.

In many applications
you can also select the blank space
▮▮▮▮▮▮▮▮▮▮▮▮▮▮▮▮▮▮▮▮▮▮
between the lines to delete it.

Also, since these blank spaces are characters, you can actually change the size of them (font size, that is), as well as the *leading* (space between the lines), the style, the paragraph spacing, etc. This comes in handy for manipulating space.

Centering Text

And a most important thing: when you **center** a word or line, Mac takes all those blank spaces into consideration, so any spacebar spaces or any first-line indents or any tabs you've inserted will be used to calculate the center of the line, making the line not *appear* centered.

I hit the Tab key before I typed the first word in this centered line. The line appears not to be centered.

This line is centered.
This line is also centered
but it includes a tab.

The invisible tab character
that is disrupting the alignment
must be highlighted
and removed, like so:

I selected the tab space to delete it.

This line is also centered.
Then it will be centered just fine:
This line is also centered.

After I deleted the invisible space, the line centered just fine.

Changing Fonts (Typefaces) and Rule #2

Throughout the entire Mac environment, to make any changes you must follow Rule #2:

Select First, Then Operate

For instance, to change to a different **font,** or typeface: first *select* the type you want to change (press-and-drag over the word/s), then *choose* the font name you want to change it into. The font list is found in your menu under various labels, depending on your program.

Notice that the insertion point picks up whatever font and style and size and alignment *is directly to the left of it.* No matter where you set it down, you will type in the font, etc., of that character, even if that character is an empty space (unless you proceed as in the following paragraph).

Now, let's say you know that the next thing you're going to type is going to be in a different font. Do you need to type it first and then select it and change the font? No.

Set your insertion point down where you want to type in the new font. *With no text selected,* go up to the menu and choose the font (and style and size, if you like); when there is no text selected, all the formatting *gets poured into the insertion point*—whatever you type next will be in the font you just chose. As soon as you place the insertion point elsewhere, though, it will again pick up all the formatting of the character to its left.

Please see Chapter 18 for more information on fonts.

Style is referring to whether the type is plain, bold, italic, outline, etc. To change the style of the type, you need to follow Rule #2: *select first, then operate.* Select the type you want to change (highlight it), then choose the style you want from the menu. You can choose more than one of these; for instance, you can have a face that is bold-italic-outlined-shadowed type. Yuk.

Changing Style

> To remove all of the style choices at once, simply select the text and choose Plain or Normal.

As mentioned in that last section about changing *fonts,* you can choose the style you want from the menu *before* you type it (as long as you don't move the insertion point after choosing). But even that's a pain if you just want to italicize the next word and then return to normal text. This is an easier method:

Notice the keyboard shortcuts in the style menu? They are almost always Command **B** for Bold, Command **I** for Italic, etc. (Some programs may use Command Shift B and Command Shift I, etc.).

Changing Styles Mid-Stream—Without Using the Menu

> As you're typing along, simply press Command **B** and the next word you type will be **bold**; when you want the next word to be *not* bold, press Command **B** again and it will take *off* the bold (that's called a *toggle switch,* when choosing the same command turns that command off). Logically, you can press Command **B I** to create a word that is (guess!) ***bold italic.***

Size in type is measured in *points.* Points, in the traditional type world outside of personal computers, are each $\frac{1}{72}$ of an inch. The Macintosh developers were brilliant in designing the Mac screen so each pixel, or dot on the screen, is $\frac{1}{72}$ of an inch—type sizes are quite true to what those who deal with traditional type are accustomed.

Changing Type Size

In your menu you see different numbers referring to the size of type; logically, the bigger the number, the bigger the type. Again, to change the size: *select first, then operate.* Or set your insertion point down and choose the size from the menu *before* you type (see the last two sections on changing fonts and styles). For more information on type sizes, see the next chapter on fonts.

Alignment

Alignment refers to where the margins are lined up: *align left* has the left margin lined up; *align right* has the right, obviously; *align center* has everything centered on a vertical axis *between your margins; justified* has both the left *and* right margins lined up. To change your alignment, you know what to do! That's right: *select first, then operate*—highlight the text, then choose the alignment.

A note when centering: If you have a first-line indent or tabs in the text that is to be centered, or if you have inserted blank spaces either before or after the text, then those spaces are taken into consideration when centering (see page 44). Also, *alignment affects the entire paragraph;* it is not possible to make one line align left and another align right in the same paragraph. There must be a hard Return separating the lines.

Cut, Copy, and the Clipboard

Almost anywhere you can type, you can cut or copy text. When you **cut** text, it is *removed* from your document and placed on the Clipboard. When you **copy** text, the original *is left on your document* and a *copy* of it is placed on the Clipboard. Well, what the heck is the Clipboard?

The Clipboard: The Clipboard is a little "container" somewhere in the depths of the Mac. In some programs you can ask to *Show the Clipboard,* in which case it appears as a window with its contents displayed. In most programs, though, you never see it; you just must trust that it's there. (If you have the Clipboard system icon in your System Folder, then it's there in every application.)

The Clipboard holds whatever you have cut or copied, be it text, spreadsheet data, graphics, etc. Once something is on the Clipboard, it waits there until you paste it in somewhere (you'll get to that in the next paragraph). **The most important thing to remember about the Clipboard** is that it holds *only one thing at a time;* that is, as soon as you cut or copy something else, whatever was in the Clipboard to begin with is *replaced* with the new selection.

The Clipboard appears as a window (if it's available for looking at)

Items will stay on the Clipboard even when you change applications; you can put something on the Clipboard in a paint program, then open up a word processing program and paste it into a new document. Items will leave the Clipboard all by themselves if the computer is turned off or if there is a power failure; the contents are stored in RAM, so anytime RAM gets wiped out, so do the contents of the Clipboard. (RAM info on page 51).

Cut

How to Cut: Simply select, then operate; that is, select the text you wish to remove from the document (press-and-drag over it). Then from the Edit menu choose "Cut." The text will be *eliminated* from your document and placed on the Clipboard. (Be sure to read "Delete" further on in this section.)

Copy

How to Copy: Simply select, then operate; that is, select the text you wish to copy (press-and-drag over it), then from the Edit menu choose "Copy." The text will *remain* in your document and a *copy* will be placed on the Clipboard.

Paste

OK—it's on the Clipboard. Now what? Well, the Clipboard holds objects for **pasting.** You can take text or graphics out of one place and paste it into your document some-where else, just as if you had a little glue pot.

How to Paste Set the insertion point where you want the Clipboard item to appear; from the Edit menu choose "Paste." In most programs, whatever was on the Clipboard will be inserted in your document *beginning at the flashing insertion point.* You can also select a range of text; the pasted item will *replace* what was selected. Spreadsheet data, graphics, etc., all can be pasted in also. In some programs, the pasted object will just land in the middle of the page.

As long as something is on the Clipboard, you can paste it in a million times.

Backspace/
Delete
or Clear
and the
Clipboard

Now, **Backspace** or **Delete** is a little different: if you hit this key (upper right of keyboard) while something is selected, whatever is selected is *deleted* and is *not* placed on the Clipboard. This means it won't replace what you have on the Clipboard, if you are saving something there to paste in again, but it also means that you don't have it anymore—it is really gone. **Clear,** sometimes found in the Edit menu, does the same thing.

Undo

Undo can sometimes save your boompah (no, that's not computer jargon—it's Grandma's euphemism). When you do something that makes you scream, "Aack! Oh no!" then try Undo. It's always the first command in the Edit menu (or press Command Z).

What Undo can undo is *only the last action that occurred.* For instance, if you selected two paragraphs of brilliantly witty text that you spent three hours composing and just then the cat walked across your keyboard and obliterated the entire work, Undo could give it back to you **IF** you asked to Undo before you touched anything. If you start fiddling around with the keys and the mouse, then what you will undo is that fiddling around. So if something goes wrong, don't scream—**UNDO.** Then scream if necessary.

Command Z X C V

Thoughtfully, the Mac designers have made the keyboard shortcuts for the cut/copy/paste/undo commands very handy. Notice on your keyboard the letters **Z, X, C,** and **V,** all in a row right near the Command key.

- ▾ Command **Z** will Undo (the closest to the ⌘ key).
- ▾ Command **X** will Cut (X like eXiting or Xing it out).
- ▾ Command **C** will Copy (C for Copy, easy mnemonic).
- ▾ Command **V** will Paste (V because it is next to C).

It's nice to get familiar with these. Remember, select first (*except to Undo*); then hold down the Command key and lightly tap the other letter.

Accessing
Special
Characters

Special characters are the symbols you have access to on the Macintosh that aren't available on a typewriter, such as upside-down question marks for Spanish (¿), the pound symbol for English money (£), the cents sign (¢), the registration or trademark symbols (® ™), etc. You can view all these with your **Key Caps** desk accessory. (If you aren't sure what Key Caps is, please read page 84.)

To get special characters into your document, follow these steps:

▼ While working in your document, pull down the desk accessory Key Caps from the Apple menu (far left; press on the apple).

▼ From the Key Caps menu (a new item that appears in your menu bar!) choose the font you wish to view.

▼ Find the character you want by pressing Shift **or** Option **or** Shift-Option together; press the character key; notice what combination of keystrokes produces the character you want. For instance, Shift Option ~ (tilde key) in the font Geneva will produce a bunny rabbit: 🐇

▼ So *remember* that keystroke combination; close Key Caps to get back to your document (remember, you can access desk accessories in any program).

▼ In your document, click to set your insertion point. Choose the font Geneva and the size 12 point; press Shift Option ~. The bunny will appear!

Another way to accomplish this is to press Shift Option ~ in whatever font you are currently using; some strange character will appear. Select the strange character and change it into Geneva 12 point; it will turn into a bunny.

You can also select and copy the character showing in the Key Caps entry bar—select as you would any text, and copy from the Edit menu. Back at your document, set the insertion point and paste it in. Unfortunately, if your document text is another font, the Key Caps characters will pick up that font. You will still have to select the new characters and change them into the font that held those characters you wanted. It seems easier just to do it the other way.

Remember, the insertion point picks up the *formatting of any character immediately to its left, even if it's a blank space,* so anything else you type will be in that character's font, style, etc. To continue in your *original* font, leave your insertion point

Using Key Caps

Some special characters and the keys to access them:

•	Option 8
©	Option g
™	Option 2
®	Option r
¢	Option $
°	Option Shift 8
…	Option ;
–	Option hyphen
—	Option Shift hyphen

Just For Fun—using Shift Option Tilde (~)

♥	New York 9 pt.
⌣	New York 10 pt.
🐤	New York 12 pt.
♫	New York 14 pt.
☭	Geneva 9 pt.
🖳	Geneva 10 pt.
🐇	Geneva 12 pt.
≣	Monaco 9 pt.
∫	Monaco 14 pt.
•:	Athens 14 pt.

A terrible thing has happened: System 7 eradicated these characters! What has Apple come to???

right where it is; from the menu just choose the font specifications you were originally using.

Using Accent Marks

A list of common accent marks:

´   Option e

`   Option ~

¨   Option u

~   Option n

^   Option i

Included in your special characters are **accent marks,** such as those in résumé and piñata. You can find them in Key Caps, but it's easy to remember that they're accessed using the Option key and are hiding beneath the characters on the keyboard that would usually be under them; e.g., the accent acute over the **e** is Option-e; the tilde over the **n** is Option-n.

To type accent marks in your document, follow these steps (using the word résumé):

▾ Type the word until you come to the letter that will be *under* the accent mark; e.g., **r**

▾ *Before* you type that letter (the letter **e** in this case), type the Option combination (**Option e** in this case) —*it will look like nothing happened.*

▾ Now type the character that is to be *under* the accent mark, and both the mark and the letter will appear together; e.g., **r é s u m é**

▾ That's easy, huh!

One Space After Periods

What?! One space after a period? If you grew up on a typewriter, this is not an easy habit to change. But characters on a Macintosh are not *monospaced* as they are on a typewriter (except for Monaco and Courier), so there is no longer the need to use two spaces to separate two sentences. Take a look at the font Courier on page 72; notice the spacing of its letters as opposed to the Times font above it. You can see why a font like that needs two spaces after periods. Check any book or magazine on your shelf; you will never find two spaces after periods (except books produced on a computer typed by someone still using typewriter rules).

A Commercial

If you are typing on a Macintosh, you must face the fact that it is not a typewriter and that some of the standard conventions developed particularly for that wonderful little appliance do not apply to the kind of type you are now creating. A very important book to read is The Mac is not a typewriter. *It's small, it's cheap, it's easy to read, and it's true. Well, yes, I did write it myself.*

CHAPTER THIRTEEN

SAVING

Saving is the process of transferring your document from the temporary memory bank where it is initially stored, over to the floppy disk or hard disk where it becomes permanent. It is *extremely important* to save your document as soon as you begin working or it, and to continue to update the save *every few minutes*.

Until you actually go through the process of naming a document and saving it, the document is stored in **RAM**, which is **Random Access Memory.** RAM is sort of like your desk, as opposed to a disk which is like your filing cabinet where you keep all your folders of information. When you are working on a project, you don't keep running to the filing cabinet every time you need a little piece of information, do you? No, you take out all the applicable info and put it on your desk, then when you're finished you put it all away again and take out something else. RAM is sort of like that: when you open an application the computer puts a copy of that application into RAM. When you close that application and open another one, Mac puts the first one back where it came from and puts the new application into RAM. That way the computer doesn't have to keep going into the filing cabinet to do its work and it can operate much more efficiently.

When you create a document, it sits in RAM, too, until you put it in the filing cabinet—your disk. You put it on your disk by **saving** it. Once it's on your disk, either hard or floppy, it will stay there until you trash it yourself.

While your document is in RAM, though, it is in **danger.** At any moment, if there is a power failure, even for a split second, or you accidentally hit the wrong button, or you have a system crash, or the screen freezes, or a virus attacks, or any other catastrophe of considerable dimension happens to befall, then everything in RAM (what is commonly called *memory*) is gone. Just plain gone. No way on earth for a mortal person to get it back.

The prevention? **SOS:** Save Often, Stupid. Well, that's a little harsh—how about Save Often, Sweetie. Save Save Save. Every few minutes, when you're just sitting there thinking about your next marvelous move, Save. In most

Saving

RAM:
Random Access
Memory

Danger!

Rule #1:
Save Often!

programs it's as easy as pressing Command S. Then if there *is* a catastrophe, you will have lost only the last few minutes of your work.

**Save As...
vs. Save**

To save a document for the first time, it must be given a name. Under the File menu are the commands **Save As...** and **Save.** At first the subtle difference can be confusing.

Save As...

Save As... is the command you must use *first* in order to give the document a name, as a document cannot be saved without a name. "Save As…" gives you a dialog box such as the one shown below (they're slightly different from program to program).

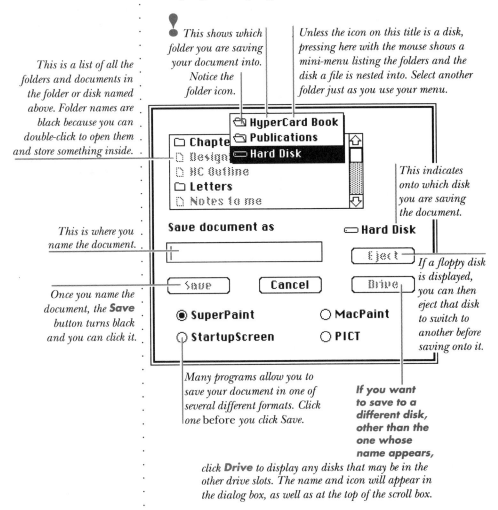

This shows which folder you are saving your document into. Notice the folder icon.

Unless the icon on this title is a disk, pressing here with the mouse shows a mini-menu listing the folders and the disk a file is nested into. Select another folder just as you use your menu.

This is a list of all the folders and documents in the folder or disk named above. Folder names are black because you can double-click to open them and store something inside.

This indicates onto which disk you are saving the document.

This is where you name the document.

Once you name the document, the **Save** *button turns black and you can click it.*

If a floppy disk is displayed, you can then eject that disk to switch to another before saving onto it.

Many programs allow you to save your document in one of several different formats. Click one before you click Save.

If you want to save to a different disk, other than the one whose name appears, *click* **Drive** *to display any disks that may be in the other drive slots. The name and icon will appear in the dialog box, as well as at the top of the scroll box.*

System 7 update: dialog boxes, page 105.

Save is the command to use *after* you have named the document and you want to save the new changes onto that same document. *Save* just goes ahead and does it— you won't see or hear anything. You must just trust.

There is no keyboard shortcut listed in the menu for "Save as…." But if you have not yet given the document a name, then choosing *Save* (Command S) will give you the *Save As…* dialog box because the file must have a name. Some programs will not even allow the name "Untitled."

If you want to create changes in a document, but want to keep a copy of the original *without* the changes, then use *Save As…* a *second* time to give the document a *new* name. This puts the original document safely away on your disk and opens a new one (the copy) right where you are. You'll notice the name in the window title bar of your document will change to what you renamed it. Any changes you make to *this* document will not affect the original.

Making Several Versions

Also, if you made a bunch of changes you don't want, simply close the document and *don't save the changes.* Reopen it and everything will be exactly the way it was last time you saved.

Reverting to the Last-Saved Version

Occasionally a program will have the option to **Revert** in the File menu; choosing this will take you back to the last time you saved, without having to close the document.

CHAPTER FOURTEEN

PRINTING

Printing is the process of copying your data that is inside the Macintosh onto a piece of paper. This piece of paper, then, in computer jargon, is called "hard copy."

Printing

There are basically two types of printers: **QuickDraw printers** and **PostScript printers.**

Printers

is a computer programming language that your *Macintosh* reads. It creates what you see on the screen. A QuickDraw printer can only reproduce what is on the screen. The ImageWriter, the HP DeskWriter, and the Apple StyleWriter are all examples of QuickDraw printers, with resolutions ranging from 75 to 400 dots per inch (the higher the resolution, the smoother the printed image).

QuickDraw printers

PostScript is a programming language that a *PostScript printer* reads. A PostScript printer doesn't care what the heck you have on your screen. If the font or the graphic image is created with PostScript, it can look dreadful on the screen but will print beautifully on the page. See the example on page 63.

PostScript printers

There are also very expensive (like $80,000), very high-end PostScript printers with resolutions of around 1000–2000 dots per inch, such as the **Linotronic.** These printers output onto film, not paper, and the hard copy looks virtually like traditional typesetting, limited only by the professional expertise of the person who input the type. This book was output on a Linotronic.

Since the high resolution machines are so expensive, you only find them in a *service bureau*—a shop where they offer the output as a service. You take the disk containing your document to them, leave it there, and they print it up for you. It can cost from $5 to $10 a page, but it's beautiful.

Printing to your personal printer is very simple. Your application may give you different print dialog boxes depending on which printer you are connected to, and the dialog boxes within different applications may look slightly different, but basically all you need to do is answer the questions they ask.

Preparing to Print

You might want to read Chapter 18 on Fonts before you print your document.

The first thing you want to do is to **Save** again—as a preventive measure always save just before you print (one never knows when the document-eating gremlins are lurking about). Also, make sure the printer is turned on (the ImageWriter must have its "Select" button on as well).

Chooser
The very first time you print on your machine, or if you are hooked up to more than one printer, or if you go

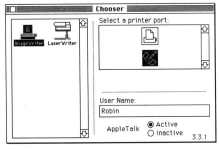

somewhere else and print, or if you find you are having difficulty printing, you need to go to **Chooser** to direct the computer to the printer.

Chooser is a desk accessory that is found under the Apple at the top left of your menu (also see page 81 for more info on the Chooser). For every printer icon in your System Folder, there will be a matching icon in your Chooser; even if you have a printer hooked-up right next to you, you won't be able to print to it unless its icon is in your System Folder.

ImageWriter icon   *LaserWriter icon*

Printer port icons. The cable to your QuickDraw printer is plugged into one of these (check the little pictures on the plugs on the back of your Mac).

On the left side of the Chooser window you will see those printer icons; click on the one representing the machine you want to print to. On the right side should be a *port* icon (asking which port, or plug, the cable connected to the printer is plugged into) or the name of all printers that are connected to your Mac and turned on; click on the one you want to use. Make sure the network button (here it is AppleTalk) on the bottom is on if you are on a network (which you would be if more than one computer is going to the same printer) and off if you are not. The LaserWriter also requires that AppleTalk be Active. Then just close the window (click its close box) and proceed.

Print Dialog Boxes
After your document is saved (and the printer is designated through Chooser, if necessary), just go up to the File menu and choose "Print...." Depending on your application, you'll get some sort of dialog box asking you questions. Most of them are self-explanatory; the following items are some terms that may not be so obvious:

> **Quality:** Draft quality on the ImageWriter prints very quickly, but eliminates any graphics you may have had and produces really awful stuff; you can generally ignore this option unless you're in an extreme hurry and don't care at all what it looks like.

You can adjust the draft quality with the button on the ImageWriter itself. If you turn off the Select light, you can push the Print Quality button to one of the three levels shown. You'll get three levels of terrible type, from awful to worse.

Orientation: Your application may use another term for it, but what the Mac wants to know is if it should print upside right or sideways (8.5 x 11 or 11 x 8.5); also known as Tall or Wide, Portrait or Landscape.

Pages: All or **From __ to __:** You can choose to print *all* the pages contained in your document, or just pages 3 through 12 (or whatever your choice is, of course). Choosing **All** will override any numbers in the **From/To** boxes.

50% Reduction: This will print your work at half size. Remember, half of an 8.5 x 11 is 4.25 x 5.5 —you must halve *both* directions. On paper, this looks like the image is ¼ the original size; it isn't—it's half of *both* the horizontal *and* the vertical.

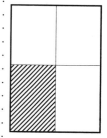

The shaded portion is 50% of the larger size— half of both the width and the length.

Tall Adjusted: The Macintosh screen has a resolution of 72 dots per inch; the ImageWriter prints at 75 dots per inch. Thus the ImageWriter tends to print large circles, such as pie charts, in oval shapes; choosing Tall Adjusted will fix that. It will also make the letterspacing more closely resemble laser printer spacing; if you're using the ImageWriter as draft copies for eventual production on a laser printer, this will help you judge the work a little better. And it looks nicer.

Computer Paper: *This does not refer to pin-fed paper!* Computer paper is 11 x 13 inches. Pin-fed paper is 8.5 x 11 (letter-size, just all strung together).

When you click the last OK button, the messages will be sent to the printer and your brilliant document shall come rolling along in a short moment.

Most laser printers spew forth a sample page every time you turn them on, useful for checking the toner level and quality, as well as letting you know how many pages have been printed since you bought the printer. If you don't want to waste paper or toner on this page everyday, simply pull the paper tray partially out before you turn it on. After a minute or two, push it back in.

Save Laser Printer Toner & Paper

Align ImageWriter Pin-Fed Paper

Most applications let you determine how far down from the top of the page you want the document to begin. Unfortunately, the ImageWriter doesn't know where the perforation of the pin-fed paper is; it just assumes the paper is aligned at the top of the pprinter and adjusts itself according to your specifications. In order to keep the printing consistent, so your documents always begin where you expect and line breaks will occur at perforations rather than in the middle of documents, do this:

1. Turn the printer on.

2. Make sure the Select light is **off.**

3. Press the line feed button until the perforation is just at the top of the printer head (if you hold the button down, after four lines it will form-feed until you let go).

4. Print your work (take notice if you need to arrange that first adjustment higher or lower; that is, above or below the printer head).

5. **When your work is finished printing, don't ever roll the paper forward manually in order to get to the perf to tear it off! That's exactly what causes the problem because then the paper isn't lined up any more.**

6. Instead, turn the Select button **off.**

7. Press the **form-feed button;** this will roll one entire sheet out of the printer, leaving the perforation lined up exactly how you just set it in step #3.

8. Turn the Select light back **on** now so you don't forget, since you cannot print with the Select light off.

9. Now you can tear off your page, leaving one full sheet hanging out of the printer.

Obviously, this is going to waste one page of paper per document. But it actually wastes *less* than if your document printed right over the perforation marks and you had to reprint the whole thing! Another good aspect of doing it this way is that with that whole sheet hanging out of the printer, the paper doesn't get curled around the roller and roll back inside itself when you try to print. You can always save the extra sheets for your kids, for scratch paper, or have the local copy shop make pads for you.

CHAPTER FIFTEEN

CLOSING/ QUITTING

When you are finished working on a document, you can choose to **close** that particular document in order to create a brand new one to work on, or to open one that has already been created. Either way, you are just *closing the document* and remaining *within the application (the software program)*. You still see the menu belonging to the application, even though the rest of your screen may look gray, just like your Desktop.

> If you don't see "Special" in your menu, or if the trash can is not there, you have not quit—you have just *closed*, but not *quit*.

Closing A Document

🍎   File   Edit   Uiew   Special

If you don't see this menu, you are not at your Desktop.

To really get back to your Desktop, where the menu items are File Edit View Special, you need to **quit** the application. This is always done from the File menu, the very last item. In most programs you can use the keyboard command: Command Q.

Quitting an Application

If you haven't saved all your changes, Mac will politely ask if you want to save them at this point, whether you are closing or quitting. Thank goodness.

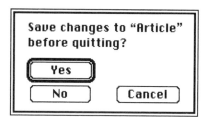

> **Save changes to "Article" before quitting?**
>
> **Yes**
> **No**   **Cancel**

If you click Yes and you haven't yet even saved the document with a name, you'll get the Save As... dialog box (page 52) to name it before quitting, because nothing can be saved without a name. Click the No button if you decide at this point you don't want the

---

System 7 update: Desktop menu, page 113; quitting vs. closing in MultiFinder, page 140.

changes (or the document, if you've never named it).
Click Cancel to return to your document without saving
any changes.

 If you hold down the Option key while choosing
"Quit," *and keep holding it down,* when you arrive at
your Desktop all the windows will be closed!

Shutting Down See page 63 about Shutting Down, if you are all done
for the day.

CHAPTER SIXTEEN

EJECTING DISKS

There are actually many ways to eject a disk, some of which are preferable to others. Let's start at the Desktop.

If you are done for the day and are planning to shut down the whole system, then close up all your windows (Command Option W for System version 6.0 or higher; make sure Caps Lock is not down). From the Special menu choose "Shut Down." This will eject any floppy disks and reassuringly notify you that it is now safe to turn off the computer.

Even if you're not ready to shut down, you may sometimes need to eject a floppy disk in order to trade it with another, or simply to take your disk and go away. Beginners usually go through the routine of selecting the disk (by clicking once on it) and choosing "Eject" from the File menu (or using the keyboard shortcut Command **E**). This will certainly work, but it is actually not the best method.

You may have noticed when you eject a disk by using the menu that a gray version of the icon stays on the screen. That's because the memory of this disk is still in RAM (see page 51). If someone else comes along to use this machine while the icon is still showing, when they insert their disk the Mac will very often spit it out and ask for the one that just left. That's not a problem if the disk is sitting right there, but if Mary took that disk and left for a meeting in Chicago, then the only thing you can do, absolutely your only option, is to turn off the computer. While that dialog box is showing "Please insert the disk "Mary"," you are stuck. Mac will accept no substitutes. If you see a gray disk icon on your screen, you can try sticking it in the trash, but oftentimes even then you'll get that dialog box. Occasionally pressing Command Period will satisfy Mac, but not often.

To avoid this problem, while at your Desktop it is actually preferable to *eject your disk through the trash*.

Aack, you say! Yes, that's a frightening thought, but calm down; it's quite all right. *The trash can doesn't erase anything off your disk.* If you simply press on the disk icon, drag it down to the trash and put it in, your disk will safely pop

Ejecting

Shutting Down
Also see page 63.

From the Menu or the Keyboard Shortcut

Gray disk icon left on the screen after being ejected.

Through the Trash

System 7 update: keyboard shortcut to eject floppy disks, page 108.

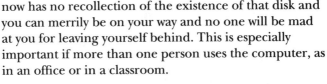

out and leave no gray icon on the screen. The computer now has no recollection of the existence of that disk and you can merrily be on your way and no one will be mad at you for leaving yourself behind. This is especially important if more than one person uses the computer, as in an office or in a classroom.

To eject a disk using the menu and leave no gray icon behind, press Command Option E, *or* hold the Option key down as you choose "Eject" from the menu.

Through Dialog Boxes Some **dialog boxes** give you an option to eject a disk while in an application: "Save As…"; "Open" in the Font/DA Mover; and "Open" in any application, to name a few. When you want to eject a disk while working, just choose something like "Save As…" even though you don't really want to rename it; choose the disk you want to eject and click the Eject button (if you don't see the name of the disk, click Drive to find it in the other drive slot). Then click the Cancel button to get back to your document.

After ejecting a disk in this way, you can of course insert a new disk if you like. If something from the ejected disk is still open on the screen, though, Mac will ask for the ejected disk again so she can put it away.

More Keyboard Shortcuts
- ▼ To eject a disk from the internal drive at any time, in any application, press Command Shift 1 (one).
- ▼ To eject a disk from the external drive at any time, press Command Shift 2.
- ▼ For a Mac with two internal drives and an external: Command Shift 1 ejects the bottom internal drive; Command Shift 2 ejects the top internal drive; Command Shift 0 (zero) ejects the external drive.

The Mouse Trick   If for some reason, perhaps because of a power outage or a system error, when you turn off the computer your disk is still inside, do this:

Hold down the mouse button; *keep holding it down* and turn the computer back on; your disk(s) should pop out like toast.

The PaperClip Trick   If all else fails, notice that tiny hole next to the drive slot? That's paperclip size. Unbend a paperclip and push it in. It's pretty safe, as all you're doing is releasing the mechanism that holds the disk in place—push firmly.

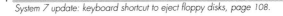

 System 7 update: keyboard shortcut to eject floppy disks, page 108.

CHAPTER SEVENTEEN

SHUTTING DOWN

Shutting down is the process of the computer tying up all the loose ends inside itself and parking the hard disk before it's turned off. You *can* turn it off without shutting down, but it's not recommended.

Shutting Down

When you're done with the Macintosh, it's **good house-keeping** to close up all your windows on the Desktop.* If you have System 6.0 or above you can press Command Option W and all the windows will fly away home (make sure the Caps Lock key is not down). If you have an earlier System version, then hold down the Option key while you close the active window; all the rest will follow.

Good Housekeeping

Once all the windows are closed, from the Special menu choose "Shut Down." All your disks will pop out and you'll get a reassuring dialog box telling you that you can now turn off your computer safely.

Turn it off with the same button you turned it on, and away you go! On any of the Mac IIs, "Shut Down" will also automatically turn off the computer.

*Alternate scenario: If you have a hard disk, then you probably need to open the hard disk window every time you turn on the computer. You can just leave that window open when you shut down and the next time you turn your Mac on, that window will be open and waiting for you.

In fact, some people like to leave often-used applications or documents right out on the Desktop where they are easy to reach, instead of in a window. Just drag the icon(s) out of their windows and make a neat little stack of them off to the side somewhere, or along the bottom of the screen. They will stay there even after you shut down. Keep in mind that some applications won't open if they can't find certain supplemental information that is kept in the original folder. If you can't open the application from the Desktop, put it back in its folder and wait until you get System 7 (see Aliases in Chapter 28, page 127).

CHAPTER EIGHTEEN

FONTS

In the Mac environment, the term **fonts** refers to the typefaces available. Technically, that's not exactly what it means traditionally, but we'll let it pass rather than confuse the issue.

Certain fonts are standard with the System that comes with your Macintosh:

Geneva	Helvetica
New York	Times
Monaco	Courier
Chicago	Symbol (Greek & other characters)
Venice	

The list is separated into two columns intentionally— do you notice anything funny about them? No? Well, it's this: one list is all **city names;** the other is not. Big deal, you say.

Actually, it is a big deal. The Mac prints to basically three sorts of **printers:** *QuickDraw printers* like the ImageWriter, with a lower resolution of about 75 dots per inch, or the HP DeskJet or the Apple StyleWriter, with resolutions of 300 to 400 dots per inch; *PostScript laser printers,* with resolutions of 300 to 600 dots per inch; and *PostScript imagesetters* such as the Linotronic, with very high resolutions of around 2000 dots per inch. *The higher the resolution, the clearer and sharper the printed letters look.* What you are reading right now is from a Linotronic.

Macintosh fonts are either *bitmapped,* designed for the low resolution of the computer screen and for printers like the ImageWriter; or *outline,* designed for high resolution like the LaserWriter or Linotronic. The city names clue you to which font works best with which type of printer.

The typefaces Helvetica and Times are very popular, standard typefaces in **traditional** type, which the Mac is emulating. Courier is monospaced and shaped like a typical typewriter font. These three, plus Greek Symbols, are installed in the Macintosh system, *as well as in most laser printers* (printers with the higher resolution of 300 dots per inch. They look very nice when printed on the LaserWriter or any of the high-end printers.

Fonts

Interesting Font Information

Printers: QuickDraw and PostScript

Note: if you want a little more in-depth explanation of QuickDraw printers and PostScript printers, see page 155 in Chapter 32 on Jargon.

Traditional Typefaces

System 7 major update: TrueType Fonts, Chapter 30, page 135.

Name Associations Now, what city do you **associate** with The Times?
New York, you say? (Actually, Times was invented for
The London Times, but we're in America, so...) How
right you are! *New York is the bitmapped, QuickDraw version
of Times.* Times has been redesigned into New York to
look as clean as possible for the lower resolution of
the Macintosh screen (72 dots per inch) and for the
ImageWriter printer (approximately 75 dots per inch).

This'll stump you—what country is the typeface Helvetica
named after? Wrong again, dear—*Confederatio Helvetia*
is what Switzerland calls herself. Do you see a font with a
city-name associated with Switzerland? Of course: Geneva.
Geneva is the bitmapped, QuickDraw version of Helvetica.

The bitmapped version of Courier (which looks like
a typewriter and why anyone would want to use a laser
printer to make their work look like a typewriter is a
mystery to me) is Monaco.

Other Installed Fonts Other *PostScript* fonts are also **installed** into the *Apple
LaserWriter* itself and into many other PostScript printers,
so if you have bought them and they are installed in your
System you can use them without any trouble.

Palatino	Bookman
Avant Garde	New Century Schoolbook
Zapf Chancery	Zapf Dingbats: ▲ ♥ ✺ ➪

(Zapf Chancery, by the way, was designed by a German,
Hermann Zapf, but modeled on an old Italian calligra-
phy. Its ImageWriter version is Venice, an Italian city.
Zapf Dingbats: *dingbats* is a technical printers'/typographers'
term referring to those little tiny pictures.)

The fonts that don't come with your System are things
you have to buy; they are often called *downloadable fonts.*
They come on a disk and must be installed into your
System with the Font/DA Mover. Apple provides a Font/
DA Mover on one of the disks that arrived with your Mac
(see Chapter 19 to learn how to work with the Mover).

**Important
Information** That's a lot of very interesting trivia, you say, but so what?
Well, the important thing to remember about all this is
the cardinal rule:

Never use a typeface with a city name on a PostScript printer.

Why Not?

What happens is the LaserWriter, or any other PostScript printer, can't read bitmapped fonts so it has to *create* them when you print. Many programs will automatically substitute Times for New York, Helvetica for Geneva, and Courier for Monaco, fooling you into thinking you have the real outline font. Have you ever seen (or produced) work on a LaserWriter where the words had awkward gaps between them, the numbers didn't line up, the tabs didn't line up, the shift-line was broken, or they looked almost as raggedy as on the screen? **That's the result of printing city-named fonts on a PostScript printer.**

Examples:

This is an example of 9 pt. New York from the LaserWriter with no font substitution.

This is an example of 9 pt. New York from the LaserWriter with automatic font substitution.

This is an example of 9 pt. Times from the LaserWriter. It doesn't need font substitution.

The bitmapped city-named fonts were designed (and actually look better than the others) for the screen and for the *ImageWriter*.

The **type size** listings in the Mac also have a little vagary that's nice to know about. Have you noticed how some of the sizes listed are in outline style (which has nothing to do with *outline fonts*), and some are not (see right)? This can be different for each font.

Type Size

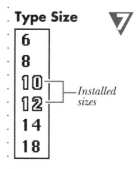

What the outlined number is indicating is that this particular size for this particular font has been *installed* in the System. It will look its best on the screen in the outlined size, and will print best on a QuickDraw printer in the outlined size. You can ask for any other size, and in some programs type in your own size up to 127 point or beyond, but it'll look funky on the screen. The bigger, the funkier. And if it looks funky on the screen, it will look funky on a QuickDraw printer because that printer can only reproduce what it sees on the screen.

Note: read about ATM and how it can improve the printing of fonts on QuickDraw printers; page 141.

A PostScript laser printer, on the other hand, can create a PostScript font *(not a city name)* in any size you like. So even if it looks totally gross on the screen, the laser printer will print it as neatly at 95 point as it will at 12 point. Note the example on the next page.

57 point Times on the screen and printed on the ImageWriter R *57 point Times printed on the LaserWriter*

If you acquire more screen sizes (or entire fonts, for that matter), you can install them with your Font/DA Mover (see Chapter 19).

Warning: technical information below

Screen fonts and Printer fonts

Fonts

The suitcase icon that holds screen fonts; used with the Font/DA Mover.

NewBasRom

Icon representing a printer font.
(ITC New Baskerville Roman)

More Examples

Simple bitmapped fonts, which are those fonts designed for the screen and QuickDraw printers like the ImageWriter and which usually have a city name, have only one part to them—the **screen font** itself. Since a QuickDraw printer prints what it sees on the screen, the *screen font* contains all the necessary information. Once the *screen font* is installed in the System (it will show up in your font list), you're ready to type and print with it.

PostScript fonts, however (those designed for PostScript printers such as the LaserWriter), have two separate parts: a *bitmapped screen font* and a corresponding **printer** (or *outline*) **font.** When you acquire new PostScript fonts, you must install the *screen font* with the Font/DA mover, just as with simple bitmapped fonts. You must **also** put the *printer font* icon into the System Folder. *Printer font icons* cannot be inside any other folder inside the System Folder or the printer won't be able to find them.

The PostScript fonts that Apple provides with the Mac and with the LaserWriter, as well as any fonts that are included in any other PostScript printer you may buy, have their printer fonts installed directly into the printer, so you needn't worry about finding and filing their printer icons.

On the following pages are examples of the fonts that are supplied with your Macintosh System, and also the other fonts that are installed in the Apple LaserWriter.

(Notice the apostrophes printed in these examples! See page 90 if you are interested—which you really should be—in how to type apostrophes and quotation marks.)

System 7 update: screen fonts vs. printer fonts, page 136.

Simple bitmapped fonts (city-named) on the ImageWriter
Faster Quality ▾ Tall Adjusted

Geneva (10 point)

Plain: The quick brown fox jumps over the lazy dog's back.
Bold: The quick brown fox jumps over the lazy dog's back.
Italic: The quick brown fox jumps over the lazy dog's back.
Bld Ital: The quick brown fox jumps over the lazy dog's back.

New York (10 point)

Plain: The quick brown fox jumps over the lazy dog's back.
Bold: The quick brown fox jumps over the lazy dog.
Italic: The quick brown fox jumps over the lazy dog's back.
Bld Ital: The quick brown fox jumps over the lazy dog.

Monaco (9 point)

Plain: The quick brown fox jumps over the lazy dog's back.
Bold: The quick brown fox jumps over the lazy dog.
Italic: The quick brown fox jumps over the lazy dog's back.
Bdl tal: The quick brown fox jumps over the lazy dog.

Chicago (10 point)

Plain: The quick brown fox jumps over the lazy dog's back.
Bold: The quick brown fox jumps over the lazy dog.
Italic: The quick brown fox jumps over the lazy dog's back.
Bld Ital: The quick brown fox jumps over the lazy dog.

Venice (10 point)

Plain: The quick brown fox jumps over the lazy dog's back.
Bold: The quick brown fox jumps over the lazy dog.
Italic: The quick brown fox jumps over the lazy dog's back.
Bld Ital: The quick brown fox jumps over the lazy dog.

Simple bitmapped fonts (city-named) fonts on the LaserWriter
no font substitution

(The lines are drawn in, as opposed to using the underline function)

Geneva (10 point)

Plain: The quick brown fox jumps over the lazy dog's back.
Bold: **The quick brown fox jumps over the lazy dog's back.**
Italic: *The quick brown fox jumps over the lazy dog's back.*
Bld Ital: ***The quick brown fox jumps over the lazy dog's back.***

New York (10 point)

Plain: The quick brown fox jumps over the lazy dog's back.
Bold: **The quick brown fox jumps over the lazy dog.**
Italic: *The quick brown fox jumps over the lazy dog's back.*
Bld Ital: ***The quick brown fox jumps over the lazy dog.***

Monaco (9 point)

Plain: The quick brown fox jumps over the lazy dog's back.
Bold: **The quick brown fox jumps over the lazy dog .**
Italic: *The quick brown fox jumps over the lazy dog's back.*
Bdltal: ***The quick brown fox jumps over the lazy dog.***

Chicago (10 point)

Plain: The quick brown fox jumps over the lazy dog's back.
Bold: **The quick brown fox jumps over the lazy dog.**
Italic: *The quick brown fox jumps over the lazy dog's back.*
Bld Ital: ***The quick brown fox jumps over the lazy dog.***

Venice (10 point)

Plain: The quick brown fox jumps over the lazy dog's back.
Bold: **The quick brown fox jumps over the lazy dog.**
Italic: *The quick brown fox jumps over the lazy dog's back.*
Bld Ital: ***The quick brown fox jumps over the lazy dog.***

ImageWriter fonts on the LaserWriter ▾ automatic font substitution

(The lines were created using the underline function; notice how awful they look, crowding the words. Also notice the awkward word spacing.)

Geneva   (10   point)

Plain: The quick brown fox jumps over the lazy dog's back.
Bold: **The quick brown fox jumps over the lazy dog's back.**
Italic: *The quick brown fox jumps over the lazy dog's back.*
Bld Ital: ***The quick brown fox jumps over the lazy dog's back.***

New   York   (10   point)

Plain: The quick brown fox jumps over the lazy dog's back.
Bold: **The quick brown fox jumps over the lazy dog.**
Italic: *The quick brown fox jumps over the lazy dog's back.*
Bld Ital: ***The   quick brown fox jumps   over   the   lazy   dog.***

Monaco (9 point)

Plain: The quick brown fox jumps over the lazy dog's back.
Bold: **The quick brown fox jumps over the lazy dog.**
Italic: *The quick brown fox jumps over the lazy dog's back.*
BdItal: ***The quick brown fox jumps over the lazy dog.***

Chicago (10 point)

Plain: **The quick brown fox jumps over the lazy dog's back.**
Bold: **The quick brown fox jumps over the lazy dog.**
Italic: ***The quick brown fox jumps over the lazy dog's back.***
Bld Ital: ***The quick brown fox jumps over the lazy dog.***

Venice (10 point)

Plain: The quick brown fox jumps over the lazy dog's back.
Bold: **The quick brown fox jumps over the lazy dog.**
Italic: *The quick brown fox jumps over the lazy dog's back.*
Bld Ital: ***The quick brown fox jumps over the lazy dog.***

PostScript (outline) fonts on the LaserWriter ▾ no font substitution

(The lines are drawn in, as opposed to using the underline function)

Helvetica (12 point)

Plain: The quick brown fox jumps over the lazy dog's back.
Bold: **The quick brown fox jumps over the lazy dog's back.**
Italic: *The quick brown fox jumps over the lazy dog's back.*
Bold Ital: ***The quick brown fox jumps over the lazy dog's back.***

Times (12 point)

Plain: The quick brown fox jumps over the lazy dog's back.
Bold: **The quick brown fox jumps over the lazy dog's back.**
Italic: *The quick brown fox jumps over the lazy dog's back.*
Bold Ital: ***The quick brown fox jumps over the lazy dog's back.***

Courier (12 point)

```
Plain:   The brown fox jumps over the lazy dog.
Bold:    The brown fox jumps over the lazy dog.
Italic:  The brown fox jumps over the lazy dog.
Bld Itl: The brown fox jumps over the lazy dog.
```

Symbol (12 point)

Plain: Τηε θυιχκ βροων φοξ φυμπσ οϖερ τηε λαζψ δογΠσ βαχκ.
Bold: Τηε θυιχκ βροων φοξ φυμπσ οϖερ τηε λαζψ δογΠσ βαχκ.
Italic: Τηε θυιχκ βροων φοξ φυμπσ οϖερ τηε λαζψ δογΠσ βαχκ.
Bold Ital: Τηε θυιχκ βροων φοξ φυμπσ οϖερ τηε λαζψ δογΠσ βαχκ.

Palatino (12 point)

Plain: The quick brown fox jumps over the lazy dog's back.
Bold: **The quick brown fox jumps over the lazy dog's back.**
Italic: *The quick brown fox jumps over the lazy dog's back.*
Bold Ital: ***The quick brown fox jumps over the lazy dog's back.***

More PostScript (outline) fonts on the LaserWriter

Avant Garde (12 point)

Plain:	The quick brown fox jumps over the lazy dog's back.
Bold:	**The quick brown fox jumps over the lazy dog's back.**
Italic:	*The quick brown fox jumps over the lazy dog's back.*
Bld Ital:	***The quick brown fox jumps over the lazy dog's back.***

Bookman (12 point)

Plain:	The quick brown fox jumps over the lazy dog's back.
Bold:	**The brown fox jumps over the lazy dog's back.**
Italic:	*The quick brown fox jumps over the lazy dog's back.*
Bld Ital:	***The brown fox jumps over the lazy dog's back.***

New Century Schoolbook (12 point)

Plain:	The quick brown fox jumps over the lazy dog's back.
Bold:	**The quick brown fox jumps over the lazy dog.**
Italic:	*The quick brown fox jumps over the lazy dog's back.*
Bld Ital:	***The quick brown fox jumps over the lazy dog.***

Zapf Chancery (12 point)

Plain:	*The quick brown fox jumps over the lazy dog's back.*
Bold:	*The quick brown fox jumps over the lazy dog's back.*
Italic:	*The quick brown fox jumps over the lazy dog's back.*
Bld Ital:	*The quick brown fox jumps over the lazy dog's back.*

No, this isn't a typographic error: Zapf Chancery is small for its size, and doesn't change styles. Neither does Symbol.

Zapf Dingbats (12 point)

Plain:	✳❈❀ ❏◆✻✳✷ ❂❐❏❰❚ ✿❑❙ ✴◆❍❏▲ ❏✿✷❑ ▼●
CAPS:	✳★✢ ✳✷☆✛☆ ✛✚✳✷✷ ◆✳✷ ❂✳✷★☆✳ ✳✷★✢✳ ✳★✢
Italic:	*✳❈❀ ❏◆✻✳✷ ❂❐❏❰❚ ✿❑❙ ✴◆❍❏▲ ❏✿✷❑ ▼●*
Outline:	✳❋❀ ❑◇✻✳✷ ❂❐❑❱❒ ✿❑❙ ✴◇❍❑△ ❑✿✷❑ ▽○

See the Zapf Dingbats chart on page 183.

Font Sizes   Below are two PostScript fonts shown in several sizes to give you an indication of what to expect in a particular size. They have been printed on a Linotronic. Times is a *serif*; Helvetica is a *sans serif*. (This book is set in 10 point ITC New Baskerville, with heads in 10 point Futura Bold.)

This line is set in 6 point Times.

This line is set in 8 point Times.

This line is set in 9 point Times.

This line is set in 10 point Times.

This line is set in 12 point Times.

This line is set in 14 point Times.

This line is set in 18 point Times.

This line is set in 24 point Times.

This line is 30 point Times.

This line is set in 36 pt.

This line is set in 6 point Helvetica.

This line is set in 8 point Helvetica.

This line is set in 9 point Helvetica.

This line is set in 10 point Helvetica.

This line is set in 12 point Helvetica.

This line is set in 14 point Helvetica.

This line is set in 18 point Helvetica.

This line is 24 point Helvetica.

This line is 30 pt. Helvetica.

This line is set in 36 pt.

CHAPTER NINETEEN

FONT/DA MOVER

A **font** is a typeface. **DA** stands for **desk accessory**, the items under the Apple menu on the far left (see Chapter 20 for more info on DAs). To move fonts or desk accessories from one place to another, like from a suitcase icon to your System, or from the System on your hard disk to a System on a floppy, you need to use the Font/DA Mover. Also use this tool to *remove* fonts or desk accessories from a System.

When you buy your Mac, a Font/DA Mover is supplied on one of the disks. Typically it's stored in the System Folder or Utilities Folder, but it can be kept anywhere you like, even on a separate floppy for occasional use.

Where do you find the fonts to install? Well, you'll notice in your System or Utilities Folder you have a little suitcase icon with a big letter A on it (you *should* have one, anyway—it may be in another folder or on one of your original disks). This icon represents the container for your screen fonts; if you double-click on it you will get the same dialog box as if you opened the Font/DA Mover.

Fonts also reside in your *System*, after they have been installed. A few are installed at the factory, and if you bought other fonts at the same time as buying your computer, the shop may have installed them for you. You cannot double-ckick the System icon to see them, though (not unless you have System 7).

To install or remove fonts or DAs, find the Font/DA Mover icon (as shown at the top of the right-hand column) and double-click on it. You will see the dialog box shown on the following page.

Font/DA Mover ▼

Font/DA Mover

Where Fonts Reside ▼

Fonts

Fonts reside in suitcase icons or directly in your System icon.

Using the Font/DA Mover

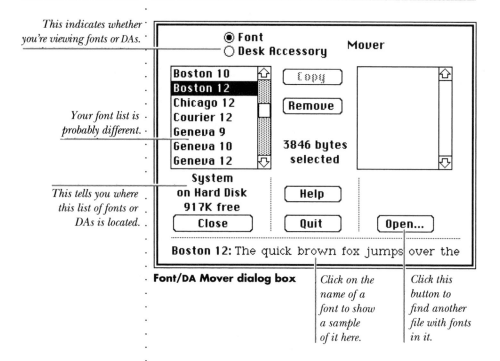

This indicates whether you're viewing fonts or DAs.

Your font list is probably different.

This tells you where this list of fonts or DAs is located.

Font/DA Mover dialog box

Click on the name of a font to show a sample of it here.

Click this button to find another file with fonts in it.

The Font/DA Mover automatically opens to show you (in the left-hand list box) the fonts that are installed on the System that is running the machine, or the fonts that are in the font file you just opened. Notice the sizes listed? Those are the ones that will show up in your applications as the outlined numbers, the sizes that are installed (as noted on page 67).

On the right-hand side is an empty box above a button labeled "Open." This side is waiting for you to open another font file so you can transfer them back and forth. So... click on the Open button to get this dialog box:

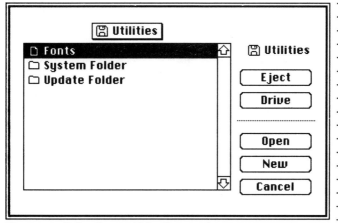

The Open dialog box within the Font/DA Mover

From this dialog box you can find the file that contains the other fonts (*Note:* The file you want may be the *System* on another disk, or the suitcase file named *Fonts,* as shown above, or perhaps it is called *Screen Fonts*):

▾ If the file is on a disk in another drive, click Drive to see it.

▾ If the file is on another disk and the current disk must be ejected to put that one in, click Eject and stick the other one in.

▾ When the file is visible in this dialog box, select it by clicking once on the name, then click Open; **or** simply double-click on the name to open it.

As soon as you open an appropriate file, you get back to the original dialog box (as shown on the previous page); this time the *right*-hand box will have all the fonts from the file you just chose.

At this point you simply select the fonts from either side that you want to copy or remove (select them by clicking once on them), then choose "Copy" or "Remove." You can use shift-clicking here to select more than one font at a time to copy—hold the Shift key down while clicking on or dragging over all your choices; they can all be copied or removed simultaneously.

Installing or Removing Desk Accessories

Desk Accessories

Macintosh desk accessories are also stored in a little suitcase icon or in the System. Accessories you buy from an outside source often have their own icon.

Installing or **removing** desk accessories works exactly the same as with fonts; just be sure to click the button at the top of the Font/DA Mover dialog box to select DAs instead of Fonts.

A Note About Families, Fonts, and Styles

Macintosh uses some of the typographic terminology in a slightly different way than traditionally, particularly in the way it defines "font." As an example, one of your fonts is named Times. Times is actually a generic *family* name; in the Times *family* you have regular, italic, bold, and bold italic; technically, each one of these *members* of the family is a separate font each with its own separate group of characters. In the Macintosh environment, when you are working with the typefaces installed in the laser printer, the *family* name, such as Times, is considered the *font* name; the variations such as bold or italic are considered *styles*. It is important to know, though, that this is a Macintosh convention, because . . .

A Note About Downloadable Fonts

When you buy fonts that are *not installed in your printer* (any font without a city name other than the ones listed in the Font chapter), you usually cannot change the *style* from the menu; these other typefaces follow standard convention and *each different style is considered a separate font* and must be treated as such. For example, if you are using Futura and want to italicize a word, you must choose the *font* Futura Italic from the font list—you cannot simply choose "Italic" from the Format or Style menu. Now, this is not always true—font technology is changing so rapidly and the standards are not defined yet and everybody is fighting everybody else for supreme font power. If you will be using typefaces other than the standard installed ones, be sure to read about and understand them—they are usually termed *downloadable* fonts, as they must be *downloaded* into the printer in order to use them. If you want to know all about Macintosh fonts, read *The Macintosh Font Book,* by Erfert Fenton.

System 7 update: installing desk accessories, page 113.

CHAPTER TWENTY

DESK ACCESSORIES

Desk accessories (DAs) are handy little tools found in your menu under the Apple, designed to make life easier. Access them like any other menu item—slide down the list until it's highlighted, then let go. They're all windows, so they can be moved around the screen from their title bars and closed with their little close boxes. They all work from within the System, so you can open any of them while you are in any application.

You can buy an amazing number of desk accessories, many for very low prices. They do all manner of useful and useless things. This list explains just the ones that come standard with any Mac.

The **Alarm Clock** won't wake you up in the morning, but it will beep at you while you're sitting at your computer. After it beeps once, the apple in the corner flashes on and off; on the newer systems it flashes from an apple to an alarm clock. The problem with this alarm is that it doesn't turn itself off—even if you turn off the computer and come back next week, the alarm clock is still flashing; you have to go get it and turn it off yourself.

When the clock is the *active window* on your screen, you can press Command C and **create a copy of the date and time;** set your insertion point down anywhere, even under an icon at your desktop, and press Command V; the date and time will paste into your document, like so: 1:38:07 AM   12/5/91.

❏ **To change the settings,** begin by clicking on the tiny flag on the right; it will open up to a little control panel. After changing a setting, click anywhere in the clock window to put it into effect.

❏ **To change the time:**
  ▾ Click on the time clock icon on the bottom left.
  ▾ Click on the number in the middle panel that you wish to change (this will cause little up and down arrows to appear on the right).
  ▾ Click on the arrows to move the time forward or backward **or**
  ▾ You can *type* in the numbers once you select them, either from the keyboard or the keypad.

Desk Accessories

Alarm Clock

| ☐   2:02:10 PM 🏳 |

Press on the numbers to drag this clock anywhere on your screen.

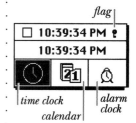

flag

time clock   *alarm clock*
calendar

Arrows with which to change the numbers

The switch to turn the alarm on or off

▼ Change the AM or PM notation the same way.

▼ *Note:* you can press the Tab key to move the selection from hours to minutes to seconds, etc.

❏ **To change the date:**

▼ Do the same as for the time, after clicking on the little calendar icon.

❏ **To set the alarm:**

▼ Click on the alarm clock icon.

▼ Change the time to when you want it to go off, as detailed above (check the AM or PM notation).

▼ Click the little switch on the *left* to the up position (you'll notice the zingers around the icon now).

▼ When the alarm goes off, you'll get a beep and/or your menu will flash, and the little apple in the menu will flash on and off.

❏ **To close up the clock:**

▼ To just get rid of the control panel, click on the flag in the upper right again.

▼ To put it away altogether, click in its close box.

❏ **To turn off the alarm:**

▼ To turn it off *temporarily,* but leave the alarm set for the next day at the same time, simply get the alarm clock and then click in its close box.

▼ To turn it off *permanently,* you must go in and reverse the process of turning it on; that is, click on the alarm clock icon and turn off the switch.

Calculator

The **Calculator** is a very handy item to have. It operates just like your hand-held calculator, although it has only the four basic functions. Remember, it's a window so it can be dragged around like any other window and put away with its close box. Access it in any application.

▼ Operate it with the mouse, keyboard, or keypad.

▼ If using the keyboard, make sure you use the real numeral 1 (one) and not a lowercase l (el).

▼ The division sign is the slash: **/**; the multiplication sign is the asterisk: ＊.

▼ The answer can be copied and pasted into your document using Copy and Paste from the Edit menu. You don't need to select the numbers first—if the Calculator is the active window, the Copy command knows what to copy. You can also copy numbers from your document and paste them into the Calculator.

The **Chooser** is where you choose which printer you wish to use. If you are working from a hard disk at home or at work and are hooked up to only one printer, or if you always use the same System disk in the same computer, you need to do this only the very first time you print.

Chooser

❑ Choose the icon for your printer:
  ▾ In the left-hand box you see the printers whose icons are in your System Folder;
  ▾ Click on the icon of the printer you are going to use (in this example it's the ImageWriter).

❑ Click on the name or the port icon of your printer:
  ▾ Depending on which printer icon you choose on the left, in the right-hand box you'll see either names of the printers available, or port icons (the port icons are asking to which *port,* or *plug* on the back of the Mac, your printer is connected). In the example you see the choice of a printer port or a modem port (here the modem port is chosen, as my *Laser*Writer is plugged into the printer port).

❑ Adjust the network option (a network lets more than one computer talk to the same printer; in this example it's AppleTalk):
  ▾ If yours is the only Mac hooked up to an Image-Writer, then AppleTalk will most likely be *inactive;* if several computers are sharing the same printer **or** if you are connected to a LaserWriter, then AppleTalk should be *active.*

❑ If you type your name in the "User Name" box, you will then have the pleasure of seeing your name on the screen.

❑ Click the close box and continue to print.

The **Control Panel** allows you to customize the Mac to your own specific preferences, such as what kind of sound to make and how loud it is, how fast the insertion point flashes, the pattern of your Desktop, etc. What your particular Control Panel has in it depends on what System you are using and what is inside your System Folder.

Many of the items are self-explanatory—just click on the radio buttons or on the numbers or on the

Control Panel

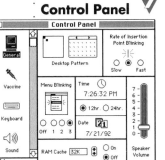

System 7 major update: Control panels, page 123.

words in a scroll box to alter things to your fancy. Here are a few specifics for areas that may not be so obvious:

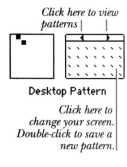

Click here to view patterns | |

Desktop Pattern

Click here to change your screen. Double-click to save a new pattern.

❑ **Desktop Pattern**

▼ On the "Desktop Pattern" click on the tiny right and left arrows—this will take you through a variety of patterns; when you like one, click on the pattern *under* the arrows and your Desktop will change. When you find the blank pattern, draw in it with the mouse to create your own—clicking on a white pixel turns it black; clicking on a black pixel turns it white, "erasing" it. All patterns can be edited.

❑ **Clock & Calendar**

▼ Setting the time and date here will change the Alarm Clock desk accessory also, and vice-versa.

Keyboard

❑ **Keyboard**

Key Repeat Rate	Delay Until Repeat
○○○◉○	○ ○◉○○
Slow Fast	Off Long Short

▼ Every key on the Macintosh keyboard will repeat, meaning if you hold the key down it will continue typing that character across the page. With the **Key Repeat Rate** panel you can control how fast it types that character across the screen.

▼ With the **Delay Until Repeat** you can turn *off* that function, so the keys will *not* repeat when you press.

▼ **Long** to **Short** gives you control over *how long* you can hold your finger on a key before it starts to repeat. This is wonderful for people who are heavy on the keys—set it for a long delay so if your fingers dawdle on the keys you won't end up with extra characters all over the place.

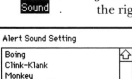

Sound

❑ **Sound**

▼ Just click on one of the sounds in the list box on the right and you'll hear it at the level that you set

Alert Sound Setting
Boing
Clink-Klank
Monkey
Simple Beep

7 –
6 –
5 –
4 –
3 –
2 –
1 –
0 –

Speaker Volume

your volume control. Whichever sound you choose last will be the one you hear whenever Mac wants to beep at you. If you don't want to hear *any* sound, set the speaker volume to zero—your menu bar will flash instead.

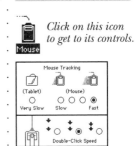

Click on this icon to get to its controls.

❏ Mouse

▾ The slower you set your mouse tracking speed, with Tablet being the slowest, the farther you have to move the mouse in connection with its response on the screen. In other words, if you have a very small space for your mouse to move around in, then set this to the fastest speed—the pointer will move farther on the screen with the minimal amount of movement on the mouse pad.

Find File

This is a most wonderful tool. There is a little man in **Find File** who will find you anything you want, even if you have no idea where it is or its exact name. The file may be in a folder which is in a folder which is in a folder. Well, this guy will go get it—he'll look in every folder on your hard drive *or* only in the folder or disk of your choice. He *won't* look in your refrigerator or under the sink.

The particular file selected here ——— is in a folder called Works Samples, which is in a folder called Works, which is in a folder called Programs, which is on the Hard Disk.

He'll not only find your file, but if you ask him nicely he will put it on the Desktop for you. Then when you're all through and don't remember where it came from, just call him up and he will come right over and put it away for you, right back where it came from. What a guy.

❏ To locate a file:

▾ The insertion point is flashing; you need to type at least three letters of the file name you want (actually, you can search with only one letter, but if there are too many files with that letter in it you will get a message telling you to be more specific).

▾ If necessary, click on the name of the disk shown in the upper left of the window to search another drive.

▾ Click on the little man **or** press Return.

▾ Stop the search at any time by clicking on the stop sign with the hand on it.

▾ The names of any files found *with those consecutive letters in the name* will be listed in the window.

▾ Click on the name of the file you want (if the scroll bar is gray, press the arrow to see more found files). In the bottom right you will see exactly where the selected file is located. Make a note of where it is.

❏ Put the file on the Desktop:

▾ You can now either close Find File and go get your

file, **or** go up to the menu bar—notice you have a new item: Find File.

▾ Choose "Move to Desktop..." to have the file pulled out of its folder and placed on the Desktop.

❑ **Put the file away:**

▾ Later, at your Desktop, when you want to put that particular file away and you don't remember where it came from, select it (click once on it) and choose "Put Away" from the File menu; the little man will come and get it and put it away for you.

❑ **From inside an application:**

▾ If you're working on a job inside a program, then pull down Find File and enter a name in the box.

▾ Click on the little man, then click on the name of the file you want.

▾ Close the Find File window.

▾ Now when you go to the File menu in your application to Open a document, the file you found will be waiting for you!

Key Caps

Key Layout

This is the icon that must be in your System Folder in order to view the special characters.

If the icon Key Layout is in your System Folder, then **Key Caps** can show you the keyboard layout for every font in your System. On a Macintosh keyboard you actually have four separate sets of keys, two of which you know already and two of which only a few people know about. You are about to become In The Know.

▾ After you open up Key Caps, you have a new menu item on the far right: Key Caps.

▾ Pull down the Key Caps menu—this is a list of the fonts that are installed on your System;

▾ Select the font you want; the characters of that font will appear on the keyboard (these are the characters everybody knows about).

▾ To see the Shift characters, press the Shift key (everybody knows these, too).

▾ To see the Option characters, press the Option key (Ha! You are now In The Know).

▾ To see the Shift Option characters, press the Shift and Option keys simultaneously.

Different fonts have different characters in the other two keyboards—some have more, some have less. Most of the

System 7 update: Key Caps, page 108.

Option key characters are consistent in every font, so you can always find, for instance, the accent marks or copyright, trademark, and monetary symbols, etc., in the same place.

Use Key Caps for finding characters

Key Caps is only for finding the *placement* of all the available characters on the keyboard. Hold down the Option key, for instance, and note where the ¢ sign is located. Once you discover that it is found under the 4 (the $ sign, logically), then you can go back to your document and press Option and 4; the ¢ will appear. It's exactly the same idea as pressing Shift 8 to get an asterisk!

Copy & Paste

It's possible to type the characters on the Key Caps keyboard, copy them (select the characters first, then choose Copy from the Edit menu), and then Paste them into your document (they will paste in wherever the insertion point is flashing). This works fine as long as the font you are using in your document is the same font you chose from Key Caps, or at least that they share the same character. Otherwise when you paste the character it will take on the *format* (type font, size, style) of the character to the left of the insertion point, which may not be what you want at all.

- ▼ At the Key Caps keyboard, find the character you want to use;
- ▼ remember what font and what keys to press to get that character;
- ▼ go back to your document, select the font you want, and press the appropriate keys;
- ▼ can you find the apple?

Also see pages 48–50 for more info.

Very interesting—this apple won't print on an imagesetter.

The **Note Pad** is a nice little feature that allows you to write up to eight pages of notes. This is a great place to leave prearranged messages, notes about particular formatting used in a document, reminders, or more love notes. They are automatically saved (they will *not* be destroyed on rebuilding the Desktop, as Get Info notes will, page 31).

Note Pad

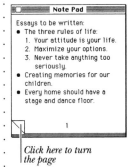

Click here to turn the page

The insertion point is flashing; type into it just as you type anywhere else in the Macintosh. You can backspace/delete, cut, copy, paste, etc. Turn the pages by clicking on the little turned corner on the bottom left; click on the *very* bottom corner to turn the pages backwards.

Scrapbook

The **Scrapbook** is a place where you can store text or graphics permanently from virtually any program; then in any other program you can take a copy of it back out from the Scrapbook and paste it into your document. Once you put something in the Scrapbook it is saved to your disk automatically. The Scrapbook holds the entire object or text, even though you can't always see all of it in the window.

See pages 46–47 if you want more information on the Clipboard.

You must go through the Clipboard to put items into the Scrapbook and to take them out.

❑ **To paste something into the Scrapbook:**

 ▾ From your document, *select* and *copy* the item you want to place (this puts a copy on the Clipboard).
 ▾ Open the Scrapbook.
 ▾ Paste the item into the Scrapbook (from the Edit menu choose "Paste")—it will be pasted onto the page that is visible, and everything else *will move over one; nothing is being replaced.*
 ▾ Close the Scrapbook to get back to your document.

❑ **To copy an item out of the Scrapbook:**

 ▾ Open the Scrapbook.
 ▾ Scroll through until the item you want *is visible.*
 ▾ Copy it (from the Edit menu choose "Copy").
 ▾ Close the Scrapbook.
 ▾ Go to your document and paste it in (usually any text that is pasted, and sometimes graphics, will insert itself wherever the insertion point is flashing; in some programs it will just be pasted into the middle of the page).

❑ **To delete an item from the Scrapbook:**

 ▾ Scroll through until the item you want is *visible.*
 ▾ From the Edit menu choose "Clear" (Clear removes it from the Scrapbook without putting it on the Clipboard).

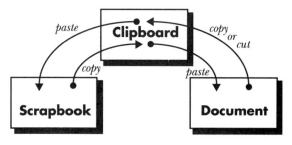

CHAPTER TWENTY-ONE

A FEW EXTRA TIPS

This is a collection of the tips or important notes that are imbedded in the rest of the book, as well as any other hints or fascinating bits of information or shortcuts that haven't been mentioned. Again, nothing is software-specific; it all relates to the general Mac environment.

Caps Lock does not act like a typewriter Shift-Lock in that you can still type numbers while Caps Lock is down. p.20

To **move a window without making it active,** hold the Command key while pressing-and-dragging in its title bar. p.22

To **align all icons horizontally** with no empty spots, hold down the Option key while choosing "Clean Up" from the Special menu. p.25

To **close all the windows** on your Desktop, hold down the Option key while clicking in the close box of the active window. p.25

On Systems 6.0 and above, you can also **close all the** by pressing Command Option W. p.25

To **close all windows on the Desktop before you even get there,** hold down the Option key while choosing "Quit" from any program. p.25

To **make the previous window close instantly,** hold down the Option key while opening folders. p.25

To **print the contents of the active window** on the ImageWriter, press Command Shift 4. p.26

To **print the entire screen** on the ImageWriter, press Caps Lock down and Command Shift 4. p.26

To bring the **window belonging to a gray icon** to the front, simply double-click on the gray icon. p.29

To **avoid the dialog/alert box** asking if you really want to throw away that application, hold down the Option key while trashing the icon. p.30

After trashing an icon, "Empty Trash" from the Special menu in order **to free that space on the disk.** p.30

Compendium of Tips

The page number indicates where more information on that tip can be found.

To **create a MacPaint file (a screen dump)** of anything on your screen, press Command Shift 3. p.30

To **write notes on a file,** use the Get Info box. p.31

To **throw away a locked file,** hold down the Option key. p.32

Use folders to organize your Desktop and all your disks as you would your filing cabinet. Chapter 9 (p.33)

Create a new folder at your Desktop *before you begin* a project and **save all your related parts into that folder,** preventing them from getting misplaced. p.35, 52

To **select more than one icon** at a time, press-(in any *blank* area)-and-drag the pointer; a *marquee* will appear. Anything enclosed in this marquee will be selected. To **move all the items at once,** press in any *black* area (except on the name) and drag; all the outlines will move simultaneously. p.38

Another way to **select more than one icon,** especially when the icons are not near each other, is to press the Shift key while clicking on icons and every one you click will be selected. Conversely,   any icon by pressing the Shift key—only the ones you click will be deselected from the group. p.38

To **copy** an icon into another folder **on the same disk,** press the Option key while moving the icon. p.38

Never hit the Return key while typing unless you really do want the line to end at that word. p.42

If you are going to **center a line ,** don't use tabs or indents or spaces before or after the line or they will make it appear off-center. p.44

While typing, **the insertion point picks up the formatting** of the character to its left—font, style, size, alignment, and ruler settings. p.44, 45, 49

To **remove all the styles** attached to characters (bold, italic, shadowed, etc.), simply select the text and choose Plain or Normal. p.45

To **change the type style** (to italic, bold, etc.) of the next word(s) to be typed, **use the keyboard commands** Repeat the command to take change the style back to normal. This avoids having to select the word(s), pick up the mouse, use the menu, and set the insertion point again to continue. p.45

Don't forget about **Undo!** If something happens that you didn't want to happen or don't like, *before you do anything else,* **UNDO** (from the Edit menu, or Command Z). p.48

To **place accent marks over letters,** use the Option characters. p.50

Use **only one space between sentences!** p.50

Never use a **typeface with a city name** on a PostScript laser printer. p.66–67

When saving, be sure to **save directly into the folder** you created to store your work. p.35, 52

Make **several versions of your work** using "Save As...." p.53

If you **change your mind about the changes** you just made, close the document and don't save those changes; when you reopen it, the document will have reverted to the last-saved version. p.53

To **avoid wasting paper and toner** every time you turn on your laser printer, pull the paper tray out a bit before you turn it on. p.57

When **ejecting disks at your Desktop,** rather than ejecting them with the menu command it is preferable to drag them out through the trash can. Or select the disk icon and press Command Option E. This doesn't destroy any data on the disk, and removes the memory of that disk so the computer doesn't ask for it again. p.62

If a **disk is stuck in the computer** after the computer has been turned off, hold the mouse button down while you turn the machine back on; the disk will pop out. p.62

As a **last resort to eject a disk** stuck in the computer, unroll a paperclip and push it in the tiny hole to the right of the drive slot. This will release the mechanism and pop the disk out. p.62

To **find a file**/document/application that somehow got misplaced but you know it's in there somewhere, use Find File from the Apple menu. p.83

Real Quotation Marks!

" and "
' and '
not " and '

Using inch and foot marks in place of the real quotation marks is an easily made mistake. Yes, on the typewriters we grew up with we used those marks, but we are no longer on typewriters. Also, we are attempting to come close to professional type, and you never see inch and foot marks used as quotation marks in professional type. Unfortunately, they are not located in an obvious spot, so you won't know they're there unless somebody tells you. So I'll tell you:

To type this mark:	Press these keys:
"	Option [
"	Option Shift [
'	Option]
'	Option Shift]

They won't always be these big round marks; each font has its own quotes designed for it. See the font lists on pages 70–73.

Return Key Shortcut

A double border around a button (such as the OK button shown below), is a visual clue that means you can press the Return or Enter keys to do that function, instead of picking up the mouse and clicking on it.

Replacing Highlighted Text

When text is highlighted, you don't need to delete it first in order to type in what you want. When text is highlighted, simply type; your typing will replace the highlighted word(s). This is true anywhere in the Mac—all dialog boxes, all programs, even on the Desktop when changing the name of an icon.

Ellipses... in the Menu

Three dots (the ellipsis: ...) after an item in the menu is a visual clue that means you'll get a dialog box if you choose that item. Anything that doesn't have the ellipsis will just activate as soon as you choose it.

Tab Key in Dialog Boxes

In any dialog box that contains boxes for you to fill in, you can press the Tab key to move the selection from box to box. If there is data already in the box, that data will be highlighted and anything you type will replace it (you don't have to delete it first). If there is no data in the box, the Tab key will set the insertion point there, ready for you to type.

On the front of the Macintosh, if you slip your hand right under the rainbow apple you'll find a little roller switch that will dim or brighten your screen. It's a good idea to dim the screen if you're going to be away from the computer for a length of time, as it's possible to burn an image into the screen, just as on video games.

Dimmer Switch

There are several varieties of "screen savers" available to help avoid screen burn. A screen saver usually turns the screen black and has images that constantly move, like shooting stars or geometric shapes or flying toasters. As soon as you click the mouse it disappears. Some screen savers are desk accessories that you access through your Apple menu; some you put in your System Folder and they automatically turn on after a certain period of time if the keys or mouse haven't been touched.

Screen Savers

Several of the paint programs allow you to create a StartupScreen. Once you have a StartupScreen installed in your System Folder, every time you boot (start the computer) with that System, this image will show on the screen for a minute or two. This is quite fun! Simply create a paint document, or use clip art, and save the document with the name "StartupScreen." It doesn't matter what letters are capitalized, but it does have to be one word. Put that file *into the System Folder.* The next time you boot, you'll see it!

StartupScreen

If you need to copy something from one floppy onto another floppy but your machine has only one floppy drive, do this:

Copying From One Floppy to Another Floppy with Only One Floppy Drive

- ▼ Insert the disk you want to copy *onto.* While it is selected (click once on it if it isn't), from the File menu choose "Eject." Remember, this ejects the disk but leaves it in RAM (p. 51). You should see the gray icon on the screen after the disk ejects.
- ▼ Insert the disk with the information to be copied *from.* Open it and select the files to copy: press-and-drag them over to the gray disk (or just drag the icon of the entire disk to the other disk, which will replace *everything*). —*continued*

▼ As Mac reads info from one disk and copies it onto the other, she will spit out disks and tell you which ones to insert next. Just follow the directions; this is called *disk-swapping*. It will eventually end.

▼ If you end up with a gray disk icon on the screen, just drag it out through the trash.

Rebuilding Your Desktop

If you have a hard disk, you may start to notice that it slows down after a few months. This is because there is an invisible file that keeps track of all the icons that have ever been seen on your Desktop, even if you just loaded them on to see what they looked like! There is a way to **rebuild** your desktop and remove all the unnecessarily stored information. Follow these steps:

NOTE:
This process will also destroy the WDEF virus!

1. Turn off the Mac (or from the Special menu choose "Restart").

2. Hold down the **Command** and **Option** keys.

3. Turn the Mac back on (if you turned it off), still holding down those keys until you see this dialog box:

> ⚠️ Are you sure you want the desktop rebuilt on the disk "Hard Disk"? (This may take a few minutes.)
>
> [OK] [Cancel]

4. Click OK (or, if you read the tip on the previous page, simply hit the Return key).

▼ **Rebuild floppy disk desktop files** the same way: hold the Command and Option keys down while inserting a disk, until you see the above dialog box.

Mac will rebuild the desktop file for you and it should now open and close files and folders much faster, plus rid it of the rude and evil WDEF virus. (Ha! System 7 is immune to WDEF!)

The only problem with rebuilding is that it also destroys any messages you put in your Get Info boxes. Darn it. (See page 31 for info on Get Info.)

Checking Your Fonts at the Desktop

To see what fonts are in the System while you are still at your Desktop, from the Apple menu choose "Key Caps." A new menu item will appear in your menu bar: Key Caps. Press on it to see your font list.

CHAPTER TWENTY-TWO

AAACK!! HELP!

This list doesn't pretend to be an all-inclusive reference for every sort of catastrophe that may befall; rather, it is just a compilation of the most common, simple problems one may encounter when first beginning to work on a Macintosh.

What To Do If:

If the computer doesn't turn on, check *all* your switches (when the switch is labeled **I** or **O**, the **I** means **On**):

The Computer Doesn't Turn On

- ▼ If you have a floor surge-protector bar with an on-off switch, it may have been kicked to the *off* position—make sure it is *on*.
- ▼ If your hard disk is external, it has its own on-off switch that must be turned on *first* so it can boot up; then the Mac must still have its own switch turned on *also*.
- ▼ If your computer has a fan unit on top with buttons to push, those buttons still won't work unless the switch on the back of the computer is *also* on. The button on the left of the fan unit typically starts the Mac, while the button on the right will start your hard disk (but the hard disk itself should be turned on first).
- ▼ If you have any other devices attached to your computer, such as a scanner, hard disk, or CD-ROM player, sometimes they must be turned on first.

You're trying to start your computer and Mac just spits out your disk and/or gives you a big X. This usually happens because Mac can't find the System Folder. If you are using an external hard disk, make sure the hard disk unit itself is turned on, as well as any extra switches. If you are using a floppy disk, the disk you are inserting does not have a System Folder on it. Or it may have a System Folder, but the System Folder doesn't contain the System icon and/or the Finder icon. *Both* icons *must* be on the disk; and actually, both icons must be in the same folder and the folder really should be named "System Folder" or confusion may result (even on a hard disk). Also, if there are any other devices attached to the computer, they sometimes have to be turned on first.

You Get the Flashing X, *or* the Disk Gets Spit Out

The Screen Freezes

Occasionally the computer screen just up and freezes. The pointer may move around, but you can't click on anything and it doesn't respond to the keys. Most often this is the result of static electricity. You can try pressing Command Period, but it usually doesn't help. Frankly, you just have to turn the machine off. Yes, you will lose everything that hasn't been saved, which is one of the reasons you should SOS (Save Often, Stupid! . . . er, Sweetie!).

Can't Find Your Document

In the beginning you may very often save a document dutifully, but then when you get to your Desktop you can't find it anywhere. This is because when you saved it you weren't paying attention into which disk and/or folder you were saving the document. Be sure to read the chapter on Saving (pages 51–53, as well as 35–36), and carefully look at the dialog boxes pictured there so you understand how to save files where you can find them again.

Anyway, at the moment you can't find it. Never fear, Mr. Find File can take care of it! Read about this guy on page 83—he'll go get your file and hand it right over to you.

When you find your document, put it in a folder you have created (page 33), just as if you were going to put it in a file folder in the filing cabinet. Press-and-drag the document icon over to the folder or disk of your choice. The folder/disk should turn *black;* when it's black, let go and the document will drop right in.

Can't Open a File

Sometimes when you click on an icon you get a message that tells you the file is locked or in use, or maybe that an application couldn't be found.

📷 14 items

This symbol indicates the disk is locked.

"Not enough memory"
to open a file?
See page 140.

If the **disk is locked,** you'll see a little lock symbol in the upper left of its window. When a disk is locked you can't save to it, nor can you print from a locked *System* disk (if you are one who still works from a floppy System disk). To unlock a floppy disk, first eject it. In one of the corners is a little black tab that covers or uncovers a hole. When the hole is open, the disk is locked (seems backwards, doesn't it?). So to unlock it, switch the tab back so the hole is closed. (More info on page 9.)

If the **file is locked,** click once on it and choose "Get Info" from the File menu. In the upper right corner there is a little box called "Locked" that may be checked.

If that box is checked, then click in the box to uncheck it and thus unlock the file.

If the **file is in use,** then it's in use. Usually you get this message if you try to open an icon that looks like a Macintosh; Mac icons are part of the System.

If it tells you **an application can't be found,** then one of two things is happening:

▼ The software application in which you created the document is not in the computer. Even though your document icon may *look* like SuperPaint, in order to view the document it has to go *into* the application SuperPaint to create itself.

▼ Some files cannot go straight from the Desktop to the application, even if the application is in the computer also. In this case, if you know the document was created in a certain application and you know that particular application is in your machine, then you must go into the *application* itself (double-click on its icon) and open the file you want from inside, choosing "Open" from the File menu.

When trying to view clip art, often you will get the message that "An application can't be found," even when the program it was generated in is on the disk. You need to open *the actual application itself,* then open each individual document through the File menu, choosing "Open" (such as MacPaint, **or** SuperPaint with the MacPaint button selected in the Open box).

Viewing Clip Art Files

If you are experiencing **system bombs** too regularly, the most common reason is that you have more than one System in your computer. One System is essential; two Systems is too many. Even though you don't see something called System Folder right there on your Desktop doesn't mean you don't have one tucked away in the depths of several other folders somewhere.

System Bombs

If you have a hard disk, don't use a floppy that also has a System on it. If the document you need is on a floppy that also contains a System Folder, *copy the document onto your hard disk, eject the floppy, and open the document from the hard disk;* you can copy the revised file back onto the floppy when you're done.

Find any extra Systems

An easy way to find all the Systems on your hard disk and on any floppy disks you are using is to ask Mr. Find File (read all about him on page 83). Move them all (except one—save the latest version!) to the Desktop and throw them in the trash. If you hold down the Option key while trashing them, you can avoid the nice dialog box that asks if you're sure you want to do this. *You won't be able to throw away the System that is booting the machine. That's good.*

Understand, though, that each System has its own collection of fonts and desk accessories. If you have customized a System Folder, save that one.

Out of memory

Running out of RAM is another prime cause for System crashes. RAM (Random Access Memory, page 51, 138) is the area in your computer where all the information is temporarily stored while you are working on it. When you Save, you send that information permanently to the disk and thus free up that much space in RAM. If you don't save very often, RAM gets full and the Mac just checks out (crashes). If you have a lot of INITs (page 148) or fonts, remember that those get loaded into RAM as soon as you turn the computer on. Then your application gets loaded into RAM. Then as you work, there is not a great deal of room left. So the moral is: Save often. If you run out of RAM often, buy more (in the form of SIMMS, page 158). Also decide whether you *really* need all those INITs and fonts and eliminate any unnecessary ones.

Desktop File is full

If the invisible Desktop File gets too large, you may run out of memory (and your computer will work slowly). At least once a month you should *rebuild your Desktop* (it's very easy; see page 92).

INIT conflicts

If you uses INITs (page 148), keep in mind that it is not unusual for them to be buggy, unstable, corrupted, etc., especially the free ones. It's a well-known fact that they can cause problems, including System crashes. If you think one of your INITs might be a catalyst for bombs, take them all out and put them back in one at a time, using your computer for several days between adding each one.

Text Formatting Unexpectedly Changed

It's not uncommon to open your document on another *System* and find major formatting changes. If you created a document on your hard disk using the font Palatino, then gave a copy of the document on disk to a co-worker who opened it up and found it had transmogrified itself into the font Helvetica and all your formatting was thrown off, that's because Palatino was not in the co-worker's *System.* If the document can't find the font in which it was created, then it has to choose another from what is available. The solution is to make sure both Systems have the fonts.

Misformatting may happen occasionally even if the fonts are the same in both Systems. Another possible reason for this is that some programs create a file in the System Folder that holds the formatting for the document. When you open up the document with a different System Folder, it can't find that document's formatting. If you know you are going to be taking the document to another computer, as soon as you quit creating it, go into the System Folder and find the formatting file; e.g., *Word Settings* if you are using Microsoft Word. Rename that file to correspond with the file you just created (though not exactly the same name), and put them both in the same folder.

▼ One of the most common reasons why printing won't work is because the appropriate printer icon wasn't chosen. Go to Chooser from the Apple menu and choose your printer (see pages 56 and 81).

▼ Make sure the printer is on, that it has paper, and that the paper tray, if there is one, is firmly attached.

▼ Make sure any networking cables are connected.

▼ On an Image Writer, make sure the Select light is on. It *must* be on in order to print.

▼ Also on an ImageWriter make sure the lever on the hand roller corresponds to the way you are feeding paper—that is, friction-feed for single sheets (that's the symbol with two rollers, towards the back); and pin-feed for pin-fed labels and paper (that's the symbol with one roller and little pins, pulled towards the front).

▼ If the disk that the *System Folder is on* has less than about 15K available, Mac cannot print. She needs some free space to send over the messages for printing. You will have to free up some space on that disk by removing a file or two.

Printing Doesn't Work

▼ Sometimes gremlins prevent printing properly. If you have checked everything and there really seems to be no logical reason for the file not to print, go away for a while, let someone else print to that printer, shut down, come back later, try again. This sometimes works. One never knows.

▼ Unusual printing problems are a common symptom of a virus attack. See page 163 for a brief explanation of viruses. If you think you have the WDEF virus, read about rebuilding your Desktop to destroy it, page 92.

Can't Form-Feed or Line-Feed the ImageWriter Paper

If you want to form-feed or line-feed the paper, the Select light must be *off.* Be sure to turn it back on again before you try to print!

Notice that the line-feed button will feed the paper through one line at a time for four lines, then it turns into a controllable form-feed; as soon as you let go it stops. Form-feed itself will roll through an entire page length (generally 11 inches).

There's Garbage Hanging Around Outside the Trash Can

If garbage piles up around your can, it's because you didn't put it *inside* the can, but set it down *outside,* just like the kids. When the *very tip of the pointer* touches the can and turns it black, that's the time to let go. *It doesn't matter if the icon you are throwing away is positioned over the can*—it's the **pointer tip** that opens the lid.

Gray Disk Icon is Left on the Screen

A gray disk icon can mean one of two things, either it is open or it is in RAM.

If the disk itself is still in the floppy drive, then the gray shadow only means that you have already double-clicked on it and its window is open somewhere on the screen. If you can't see the disk's window because there are other windows in the way, simply double-click on the gray shadow and it will come forth as the active window.

Gray disk icon left on the screen after being ejected

If the disk itself is not in the floppy drive, then you most likely ejected that disk by choosing "Eject" from the File menu or by pressing Command E. This procedure does eject the disk, but also leaves its information in the Mac's *memory.* Read page 61 for an explanation of what happened and how to avoid it.

PART II

SYSTEM 7

You've heard about it. Do you want it? Do you need it? You may have it. If you don't, should you get it? Is it worth it to become, as they say, System 7–savvy?

Whether you should make the upgrade to System 7 depends on what kind of Mac you have and what you want to do with it. You need a Mac with a hard disk and (they say) 2 megabytes of RAM. That includes the bigger machines like the SE/30 and the Mac II family, and it *can* include even a Mac Plus or a Classic. (RAM is different than your hard disk storage space! A typical SE has a 20 or 30 meg hard disk, but only 1 meg of RAM. For RAM info, see pages 51 and 138.)

How can you tell how much **RAM** you've got? Use the Apple menu and choose "About the Finder" (if you're running System 7, it'll say "About This Macintosh"). You'll see "Total Memory"; if it says 2000 or more, you've got the RAM you need *to run System 7*. If you happen to want to run *applications* as well, such as your word processor or page layout program, you need more RAM. With 2 megabytes you can run System 7 and probably the Calculator desk accessory. Realistically, you need a *minimum* of 4 megs of RAM.

As for whether you want it right now, consider these questions: Do you have a hard disk with at least 4 megs of RAM? Do you understand and enjoy using MultiFinder, where you can run several programs at the same time and switch between them? Are you part of a work group that shares documents on a network? Do you have several computers in your home or office that you would like to network (share files)? Do you like being able to customize your Mac and tinker with how things look on the screen? Do you have fun with sounds? Are you fanatical about keeping up with the latest, even if it's not really necessary and even if it means you'll have some inconvenience for a while until all your applications, INITs, CDEVs, and desk accessories make the upgrade? If you answer yes to all of these, System 7's probably for you. It's actually not that much different—just a few more bells and whistles.

Are Your Current Applications Compatible?

System 7 comes with a "compatibility checker"—a Hyper-Card stack that will check your hard disk and report back if you have any programs that aren't compatible with it (which means, of course, that you must have HyperCard installed on your hard disk to run the checker).

Apple classifies programs into three categories:

▾ **System 7–dependent** programs need System 7 to run. They won't work if you're using an earlier System.

▾ **System 7–friendly** programs can run under either System 7 or an older System, and they have some new features like Balloon Help that work only if you're running System 7.

▾ **System 7–compatible** programs run under either kind of System, but they don't have any of System 7's new features.

How to Get It

You can get System 7 from your computer dealer, usually for about $99, which includes documentation. You can also get it (cheaper) from a user group like BMUG (Berkeley Macintosh Users Group) at (415) 549-2684 or the Boston Computer Society/Macintosh (BCS/Mac) at (617) 625-7080. If you're not near the East or West Coast, call Apple at (800) 538-9696 for the number of a user group near you. You can download it off a bulletin board service, if you don't mind tying up your phone for hours. If you don't pay the $99 you don't get the documentation, but you can get *The Little System 7 Book* for only $12.95, by Kay Yarborough Nelson, which is better than the documentation anyway.

What To Do With It

System 7 comes on an intimidating ten disks, but two of them are previews of what you get. The "Before You Install" disk will give you a tour of System 7's new features (via a HyperCard stack) and will also check your hard disk and report whether you have any programs that aren't compatible with System 7. The "Networking Basics" disk is an overview of (you guessed it) networking concepts like file sharing; if you aren't on a network, you don't need it. So you're left with only eight disks to deal with, and the Installer program will take care of most of that for you. Just put the Installer disk in your floppy drive, double-click the Installer icon, and choose Easy Install.

CHAPTER TWENTY-THREE

BRIEF OVERVIEW

System 7, of course, has a number of interesting features that earlier Systems don't have. This chapter contains a brief overview of the main features. The following chapters elaborate on some of the biggest and most important of these.

Although a lot of the new features aren't visible at first, you will see some differences immediately on the Desktop screen. For instance:

The menu bar isn't quite the same; see page 113.

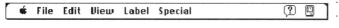

Windows, when viewed in a list, offer more information. If your windows don't look exactly like this one, it's because the viewable info is customizable; see page 123. When you view a window as a list, you see little triangle icons; see page 109.

The System Folder has many new and important folders, plus some new icons for old favorites; see page 119.

Several Immediate Visual Differences

Icons get a box around their titles when they are ready to be renamed; see page 112.

 becomes →

Icons can be customized, like this one; see page 112.

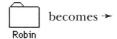

You may see aliases of any sort of file; see page 127.

Switching Programs (MultiFinder)

The Application menu.

In System 7, you are always running under **MultiFinder.** This is probably the biggest single change for users, especially those who have never used it before. On earlier systems you can *choose* to run under MultiFinder, but on System 7 you have no choice.

MultiFinder allows you to open more than one program at a time. For instance, you can open PageMaker to create a publication, then bounce into SuperPaint to make a graphic for the publication, without having to quit PageMaker.

The little icon in the upper right corner of the menu bar is the **Application** menu. When you *press* on that icon, you will see a list of all the programs that are open at the moment, and you can choose to go to another one. See Chapter 31, page 1137, for details.

Aliases

Shared Folder alias

An **Alias** is a *representation,* or fake duplicate, of an original file. Aliases let you store items where they're easiest to get at, rather than having to dig deep into nests of folders. You can put representations of your word processing program in several different folders or even in the Apple menu. (Yes! System 7 lets you customize the Apple menu.) See chapter 28, page 127, for full details on aliasing.

Label Menu

The **Label menu** provides labels you can apply to icons that allow you to organize projects or group files even if they are not in the same folder. You can search for all the icons that belong to a particular labeled category, like "Love Letters" or "Business Correspondence" or "Top Secret Star Wars," etc. See Chapter 25, page 114.

Find File

Find File is in the File menu now as "Find..." (instead of "Find File" on the Apple menu). He doesn't tell you where your file is; he actually gets it for you. He has some great new search capabilities. See Chapter 29, page 131.

Help Menu

The **Help menu** is on the far right of the menu bar, identified by the question mark icon. When you choose "Show Balloons" from the Help menu, you will see little balloons filled with information as you move the pointer across the screen. There is a separate balloon for each item you point at. See page 116.

The Trash Can

The **Trash Can** does not empty automatically as soon as you do something else, like copy a file, eject a disk, or shut down your Mac. Whatever you put in the can stays there, even if you turn off the computer, until you *choose* to empty the trash.

You can double-click on the Trash Can icon to see what's in there. Just drag a trashed file back out if you decide that you really want to keep it after all (or select the icon and press Command Y to have it Put Away for you).

When you choose Empty Trash from the Special menu, you'll see a **warning dialog box.** It asks if you're sure you want to empty the trash and tells you how much stuff is in there.

⚠ The Trash contains 8 items, which use 454K of disk space. Are you sure you want to permanently remove these items? [Cancel] [OK]

If you don't want to see this dialog box, hold down the Option key while you choose Empty Trash. Or you can suppress the warning permanently (until you choose to turn it on again):

- ▾ Select the Trash Can icon (click *once* on it).
- ▾ From the File menu, choose Get Info.
- ▾ Click the "Warn before emptying" checkbox so there is no check in it.
- ▾ Close the Get Info window (click in its close box *or* press Command W).

Desk Accessories and Fonts

Desk accessory icons can be kept anywhere you want, not just listed in the Apple menu. If you double-click on a suitcase that contains desk accessories, you'll see that in System 7 each desk accessory has its own icon. You can double-click an icon to use that accessory. To install it in the Apple menu, just put the icon in the Apple Menu Items folder, found in the System Folder (that's right—you don't have to use the Font/DA Mover). See page 113.

To install the **TrueType fonts** that come with System 7, or to install any other type of font, just drag their icons into your System file (like desk accessories, each size font now has its own icon; the icons just appear when you double-click the suitcase while in System 7). TrueType fonts look good on the screen at any size, and they look good in your printed documents, too, even when printed on an ImageWriter or an ink-jet printer. For the details, see Chapter 30, page 135.

**Desktop
(Finder)
Windows**

System 7–style **windows** are different at the Desktop. If you're viewing by Name (or by any other choice except Icon or Small Icon), you'll see a little triangle to the left of each file. You can click on the little triangle to see what's in the folder without opening a new window. This lets you find files without having to open a lot of windows on your Desktop and getting lost in the clutter. It also makes copying and moving files from folder to folder a lot easier because you can pull items out of several different folders at once. See Chapter 24, page 109.

Dialog Boxes

System 7 **dialog boxes** often display a downward-pointing arrowhead in the title above a list to indicate that a pop-up menu is lurking underneath (in addition to the standard visual clue of a shadowed border).

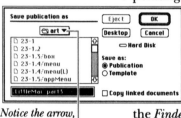

Notice the arrow, indicating this title is also a menu, as shown below.

There is a button in dialog boxes called "Desktop" instead of "Drive." To view the files that are on the *Desktop* level (also known as the *Finder* level, see page 13), click the "Desktop" button once. At this level you see the Trash Can, the icon for your hard disk, any files you have stored outside of a window, and any floppies in your floppy disk drive. To get into the floppy disk, just double-click on the name of the disk shown in the list. You can choose to Save a file directly onto your hard drive's Desktop, which means it will not be in any folder, but right there on the screen.

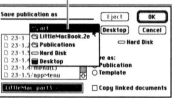

Many dialog boxes will also have a button called "New Folder." This is wonderful! If you forgot to create a file folder before you started working on the project (as I explained on page 35), you can create a folder from within the application, then save your files right into it.

Notice the double-border around the list box.

The list box itself gets highlighted with a double border when you click in it, press on its menu, or press the Tab key. While the list box is selected like this, you can type the first letter (or first couple of letters, if necessary) of a files's name to select that file. Press the Tab key again to highlight the name edit box so you can type a name for a new file.

Notice that the dark-bordered button changes from "Save" to "Open" or "OK," depending on what is selected.

OK, so maybe this isn't a change in a basic technique, but it's fun.

▾ **To switch the Puzzle** from the Apple logo to the numbers, choose "Clear" from the Edit menu while the puzzle is active. Choose "Clear" again to get the Apple logo.

▾ **To view the finished puzzle,** choose "Puzzle" from the Apple menu.

▾ From the Edit menu, choose "Copy."

▾ Put the Puzzle away by clicking in its close box (*or* press Command W).

▾ From the Edit menu, choose "Show Clipboard" to see the completed puzzle. Press Command W to close the Clipboard.

▾ **To paste different new pictures** in the Puzzle to entertain your kids or yourself:

▾ Create a graphic in your painting or drawing program, or open some clip art or the Scrapbook.

▾ Select the graphic and copy it.

▾ Quit the graphics program or close the Scrapbook.

▾ Open the Puzzle.

▾ From the Edit menu, choose Paste. Zap. A whole new Puzzle.

▾ **To get the original Puzzle back,** choose "Clear" from the Edit menu.

You can print the contents of the active window or of the entire Desktop to any printer. Both of these techniques listed below are great for when you want to keep track of the contents of a folder, of the Desktop, of your filing system, rather than writing it all down by hand. You can open the window of a floppy disk, print that window, then cut out the printed list and attach it to the disk.

▾ **Print the contents of the *active* window** (the one with stripes in its title bar): Click on the open window you want to print. Then from the File menu, choose "Print Window...."

▾ **Print a picture of the entire Desktop:** Click on the Trash Can or on any icon that's at the Desktop level (or press Command UpArrow) to select the Desktop. From the File menu, choose "Print Desktop...."

The Puzzle

The completed Apple logo puzzle. No, I didn't cheat; I really did it.

The numbers puzzle.

When you solve a puzzle, a little man congratulates you, shouting, "Ta Da!"

A custom-made puzzle.

Print the Window or the Desktop

Stationery Pads

FaxCover   FaxCover

On the right is a stationery pad made from the original PageMaker document on the left.

Click this button to create the template.

You can make a template out of any document. System 7 calls it a **stationery pad.** When you make a stationery pad out of a document, the icon looks like a sheaf of papers, as shown on the right. When you double-click a pad to open it, you'll first get the dialog box shown here so you can give the new file a name and choose where you want to store it. The original template, or stationery pad, remains unchanged, so you always have a clean master copy.

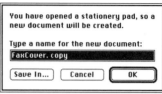

You can create a stationery pad for any document through its Get Info dialog box. At the Desktop, select the document, press Command I, and click the checkbox at the bottom of the Get Info window. The document itself turns into the stationery pad. If you don't see the checkbox, then you can't make a template out of that file. You cannot make templates of applications, folders, etc. Just documents.

Eventually all programs will have the option to create a stationery pad built right into the Save dialog box. It will look like this one shown here, from TeachText. To create the pad, click the icon that looks like a sheaf of papers.

A Few Extra Tricks

If you hate to turn on a Mac and see open windows lying all over the place, then hold down the Option key as you start the computer. **All windows will be closed** when you get to the Desktop.

INITs and CDEVs often cause problems with Systems. If you have a suspicion one may be giving you grief, **disable all extensions** (INITs and CDEVs) as you turn on the Mac by holding down the Shift key as you start. Or hold the Shift key as you choose "Restart" from the Special menu.

This is terrific: **eject a disk** with a keyboard shortcut and leave nothing in memory (see page 61 if you don't know what I'm talking about).

   ▾ Select the disk (click once on it)

   ▾ Press Command Y. This is actually the keyboard shortcut for the menu command "Put Away."

Some of System's 7's features aren't visible, and some of them have to be added to programs by the software manufacturers themselves. So the features you see will depend on the programs you use. For example, some programs can take advantage of a great feature called **Publishers and Subscribers** that will automatically find and appropriately update other related documents. Say, for example, you created a spreadsheet showing the April expenses for the bed-and-breakfast inn that you run. You want to put the spreadsheet data in a letter to your bank to show them what a great financial manager you are and thus get a bigger loan. You also want to put it in a letter to your cousin Ralph to convince him that right now is not a good time for him to move in with you. If your spreadsheet program and your word processing program have Publish and Subscribe in their File menus, you can "publish" the spreadsheet and then "subscribe" to it in all the different letters. If you later go back into your spreadsheet program and change the original numbers, the data will automatically change in the letters that subscribe to it. Wow.

Pubs and Subs

If you're part of a network, **sharing files** with other people on the network is much easier. You can store a program on one computer, yet someone on another computer can use it (read your license agreement). You can decide exactly who gets to see which files. You can lock files so no one can snoop. You can set up "drop" folders, like a message drop, to exchange messages with everybody on the net. You can access your own computer from someone else's. You even get to use passwords.

Sharing Files

If you have two or more Macs in your home or office, take advantage of the Mac's built-in networking feature. Just get a LocalTalk kit (or the PhoneNet substitute) from your favorite mail-order house, and plug in the cables. Then get *The Little System 7* book and let Kay walk you through the steps of setting up and operating your network.

Virtual Memory　With **virtual memory,** your Mac can use extra space on your hard disk as though it were RAM (see pages 51 and 138 for info on RAM). It means you suddenly have more space for opening more programs simultaneously (MultiFinder, page 137), for working with large graphics, etc. Only certain Macs can take advantage of this.

End of Brief Overview　That's the fifty-cent tour of System 7. Keep on reading for a closer look at its biggest new features, but remember, this is just an introduction. Peachpit Press has a great book, *The Little System 7 Book,* that you might want to read if you really want to get to know System 7 in greater depth.

CHAPTER TWENTY-FOUR

WINDOWS AND ICONS

System 7's Desktop, at first glance, looks just like any other System version's Desktop, especially if you're viewing windows "by Icon" ("viewing" info on page 25). You will see fancy new three-dimensional icons, though, if you have a color or grayscale monitor. And if you view any window "by Name," you'll see some big changes.

The format for viewing the contents of windows when you choose some sort of list (by Name, Kind, Size, etc.) is called **outline view.** There's a tiny triangle next to each folder's name, and if you click on that triangle you will see what's in that folder. The items contained within a folder are indented just a little from the left, as in Jimmy's folder shown here.

You can just keep opening folders within folders until you are all the way to the bottom of your filing system, with everything displayed in the same window. (If you accidentally double-click on the folder's *icon* instead of single-clicking on the *triangle,* you'll open a new window showing what's in the folder, just as in earlier Systems or just as in the Icon view.)

You can see at a glance exactly how your files are organized. You can move items from one folder to another, even if the folders are several levels apart. You can Shift-click (page 38) to select items from any number of different folders.

To **expand,** or open a folder, single-click on the little sideways-pointing triangle (or select the icon and press Command RightArrow).

To **compress** or close a folder, single-click on the downward-pointing triangle (or select the icon and press Command LeftArrow).

System   Clipboard

Fancy grayscale icons.

Outline Views

An expanded view of the entire SRJC folder.

Expanding and Compressing Folders

An expanded view of the entire SRJC folder.

Selecting Icons

While viewing a window in one of the list views (by Name, Date, Size, etc.), you can **drag to select files** that are next to each other. Press in a white space in the window next to a file name and start to drag. The selection marquee will appear when you drag, and any item that is even partially enclosed within the marquee will be added to the selection.

To **select any icon** (no matter how you are viewing the window), just type the first letter of the name of the file and you 'll be taken right to it. If there are several files with the same first letter, quickly type the first couple of letters. This makes it a lot easier to find your Word folder in an alphabetized list, for instance. Or a file that starts with Z. Or any icon in a crowded folder. You can also use the arrow keys to select files.

Zoom Box

When you click in the **zoom box** (upper right of the window, see page 22), the window will only zoom open as large as it needs to be to display all the files. If you want to open the window to as large as can possibly fit on the screen (yet still see the trash can), hold the Option key down as you click in the zoom box.

Scrolling

The window will **scroll** as you drag an icon within it. When you let go of the mouse button, the icon will pop into the nearest space in the window. Press the arrow keys to select icons, which will in turn scroll the window as well.

Active Windows

When you click on an item in a window that is not active, the window doesn't *become* active until you release the mouse button *while the pointer's still in the window.* This subtle change makes it easier to move and copy items that are in different windows; that is, you can grab an icon from an inactive window and drag it into another window without the first window popping up to the top layer. (Make sure you press on an *icon,* though; if you just click in any *blank space* in the window, the window will immediately become active and pop to the top.)

Window Shortcuts

There are a great number of tricks you can use to manipulate the windows at the Desktop (Finder). In fact, there are so many that Apple has provided several Help screens describing them, including more keyboard shortcuts than you can remember.

To view these Help screens, press on the Help menu (the question mark in the far right of the menu bar). Choose "Finder Shortcuts."

> If you don't see the "Finder Shortcuts" command, it is because you are not at the *Finder,* or *Desktop,* level. To get to the Finder, press on the icon in the top far right of the menu bar, next to the question mark, and choose "Finder." Or, if your trash can is showing, click once on it. Or press Command UpArrow.

Here's an example of a Finder window shortcut:

| To clean up and sort icons | Option + Clean Up |

> This means: If you want to clean up (align) all the *icons* that are in the *active window* and sort (alphabetize) them, then press the Option key while you choose "Clean up" from the Special menu.

Actually, there's a tricky little thing that happens here. As you probably already know, you can only clean up a window that is showing "By Icon" (whether large or small). Option plus Clean Up will sort the icons according to the last list view you chose! That is, if you choose "By Date" and *then* choose "By Icon," when you Option Clean Up the icons will be lined up by date! Try it.

> If you are viewing the window by one of the lists (Name, Size, Label, etc.), you can **switch views** simply by clicking once on another column header in the information bar.

You can also **customize** the information displayed in these columns; that is, you can choose to show just the labels, or just the dates they were last modified, etc. You can also customize the size of the icon that shows in a list view, as well as the font. Use the Views control panel for customizing (see page 123).

To **view the hierarchy of a nested folder,** hold the Command key down and press on the title of the window (not the stripes in the title bar, but the actual title itself). This displays a pop-up menu, as shown to the right. Choosing another level will open that window.

Cleaning up

Change the View

Click here to change the view to Size.

Menu of Folders

Renaming Icons

To **rename** any icon—a folder, a document, a program, a disk—just click once on the icon's *name,* not on the icon's *graphic;* then simply type the new name. A box appears around the name so you know you're changing it. Or instead of clicking on the name, you can select the icon and press Return to get that box around it. (The box and the insertion point do seem to be annoyingly slow to appear; be patient.)

If you rename something by mistake and you notice it before you press Return or click the mouse, press Command Z to Undo and get the original name back.

Creating Your Own Icons

Robin   MacPaint 2.0

No longer boring ol' folders!

You can **create your own icons** and apply them to any existing icons. This is too cool. Fairly useless, but cool.

▾ Open a graphic program like SuperPaint or MacPaint.

▾ In the graphic program, create the little picture that you want as your icon, *or* you can use any clip art or Scrapbook image. No matter what size you make it, the Mac will reduce it to an appropriate size as it becomes the new icon. (If you create it too large, though, it will be unrecognizable when reduced.)

▾ Select the image you just created or found; copy it (from the Edit menu).

▾ Quit the graphics program. Go back to the Finder (press the Application menu in the far right corner of the menu bar; choose "Finder").

▾ Click once on the icon you want to replace. From the File menu, choose "Get Info" (or press Command I).

▾ Select the icon that appears in the upper left of the Get Info window (click once on it).

▾ From the Edit menu, choose "Paste" (or press Command V).

▾ Close the Get Info window (press Command W).

Click here to select the icon.

To **change an icon back to the original,** select its tiny icon in the Get Info window and choose Cut (Command X) or Clear.

CHAPTER TWENTY-FIVE

THE MENUS

System 7's menus have a few new and interesting features.

The Apple menu has tiny icons that attempt to give you some kind of visual clue as to the nature of the item. You can customize your Apple menu by adding items to it that you use frequently. Documents, folders, programs— stick 'em in the Apple menu.

If you place a folder in the Apple menu, selecting it from the menu will open the folder for you. If you place a program in the Apple menu, selecting it will open the program for you. **Desk Accessories:** You no longer need the Font/DA Mover to install desk accessories. Your DA suitcase will open to display each desk accessory as an icon.

Follow these steps to install any file, *including desk accessories,* in the Apple menu.

- ▼ To customize your Apple menu, open your System Folder.
- ▼ There is a folder in the System Folder called **Apple Menu Items.**
- ▼ Find and select the item you want to appear in your Apple menu; drag its icon into the "Apple Menu Items" folder. The item will appear in the menu instantly; you don't need to restart the computer for it to take effect.

The Apple menu displays items alphabetically, as I'm sure you've noticed. When the Mac alphabetizes, blank spaces and punctuation are sorted in front of any other character. So if you add a blank space or a period as the first character in a name, that file will be first in the Apple menu list. The more blank spaces, the higher on the list it will be located.

You don't have to move the actual file into the Apple Menu Items folder, since you may need it elsewhere—you can move an *alias* so the *original* will stay in its own folder. See page 127 for an explanation of aliases and more suggestions for using them. They are really cool.

The Apple Menu

This Apple menu has been customized.

Apple Menu Items

Put items in this folder.

Trivia: *Hold the Option key as you press on the Apple menu. Choose "About the Finder" to see an interesting graphic (it's actually the graphic for the very first Macintosh Finder). Wait a minute or two for the secret message. If you hold down the Option and the Command keys before you choose it, you'll get a very interesting cursor in addition to the secret message.*

The File Menu

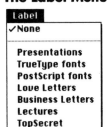

File

New Folder	⌘N
Open	⌘O
Print	⌘P
Close Window	⌘W
Get Info	⌘I
Sharing...	
Duplicate	⌘D
Make Alias	
Put Away	⌘Y
Find...	⌘F
Find Again	⌘G
Page Setup...	
Print Desktop...	

A couple of new choices have been added to the **File menu.** If you're on a network, you'll be able to use the "Sharing…" command, which lets you share your files with other folks on the network. System 7 comes has all sorts of networking features built into it. If you're not on a network, the Sharing command may be dimmed so you can't use it. See page 108 for brief information on sharing.

There's also a "Make Alias" command that lets you make an alias of the item you've selected. See Chapter 28, page 127 for full details.

And there are two hot new "Find" commands on the File menu, replacing the desk accessory "Find File." See Chapter 29, page 131.

The Edit Menu

The **Edit menu** looks just like it does in earlier Systems. As more and more programs are developed especially to run with System 7, you will be able to use the Edit menu to cut and copy text even if you have a dialog box open.

The View Menu

The **View menu** itself may not look different, but there are a couple of new tricks. There is a new **Views** control panel that lets you customize how you want your Desktop windows to look. You can choose a different typeface for the icon names, for instance, or a larger type size. You can choose what information you want displayed in the window, such as folder size and comments. See page 123 for more details, and page 111 for some good tricks.

The Label Menu

Label

✓None
Presentations
TrueType fonts
PostScript fonts
Love Letters
Business Letters
Lectures
TopSecret

The Label menu lets you assign **labels** to icons. A label is *in addition* to the icon's name (it doesn't even show up unless you choose it to be displayed in a list; see "Views Control Panel" on page 123). Labels allow you to set up an alternate system of grouping icons that are related to each other, but which may be stored in different places.

For instance, let's say you are organizing a fund raiser and you have a couple of word processing documents, a spreadsheet, and a database file all relating to the project. You can give each one a label of, perhaps, "Fundraiser." Once you have assigned labels to icons, you can choose to view your window by Label, which groups the icons of like labels together. You can also search by label, using the Find command (page 131).

The labels in the menu can all be changed; you certainly don't have to use the names Apple provides. To set up your own system of labels, use the "Labels" control panel.

The Labels control panel.

▾ From the Apple menu, choose "Control Panels" (or double-click on the "Control Panels" folder that's in your System Folder).

▾ Double-click on the file "Labels."

▾ Select an existing label (you can press Tab to select each one), then type the name of the new label.

▾ Close the control panel windows (click in their close boxes, or press Command W twice). The revised label list will instantly appear in the Labels menu.

▾ To apply a label to an icon, simply select the icon or group of icons. Then choose the label from the menu.

▾ **Note:** If you apply a label one day and then later change the name of that particular label in the control panel, all icons with the previous label attached will change to the new label! For instance, say I labeled 12 documents with the label "Love Letters." If I go to the control panel and change "Love Letters" to "Dog Food," every document that had the label "Love Letters" will now have the label "Dog Food."

The (Missing) Color Menu

If you have a color monitor, you may notice that there's no more **Color menu** to assign colors to *icons*. Use the **Labels control panel** instead (see the section above). Single-click on a color and then pick a new one from the color wheel that appears.

To assign color to highlighted text and to your window borders, use the **Color control panel** (page 124).

The Special Menu

The **Special menu** looks pretty much the same, but you may notice that the **Set Startup** command is missing.

▾ To choose a **different startup disk,** use the Startup Disk control panel: either choose "Control Panels" from the Apple menu, or double-click on the "Control Panels" folder, found in your System Folder. See Chapter 27, page 123, for details on control panels.

▾ To have an application or particular **document open on startup,** put the file (or an alias, page 127) into the folder "Startup Items," found in the System Folder.

Clean Up

The **Clean Up** command on the Special menu has several neat tricks. As always, "Clean Up" only works when you are viewing "By Icon" or "By Small Icon."

▾ Clean up *selected* icons by pressing the Shift key as you choose "Clean Up" from the Special menu. Selected icons will snap to the nearest available spot on the invisible grid.

▾ Clean up all icons into *alphabetical order* by pressing the Option key as you choose "Clean Up." Icons will snap into alphabetical rows with no extra spaces between (System 7 does allow space between icons with long names).

 Actually, it is not always in *alphabetical* order that the icons get sorted when you do this trick. They will be organized according to how you last viewed them in a list. That is, if you choose "By Label," then choose "By Icon" again, when you Option Clean Up the icons will be organized by label. Cool.

▾ If you click on one of the items on your Desktop, such as your hard disk icon or the trash can (or if you press Command UpArrow), then the Special menu will show "Clean Up Desktop." Choosing this command will make all the *icons* (not open *windows*) on your Desktop snap to the nearest spot on the underlying invisible grid. If you press the Shift key first, then only the *selected* items will snap to the grid.

 ▾ If you press the Option key before you choose "Clean Up Desktop," then all the icons on the Desktop will snap over to the far right and will line up in alphabetical order (your hard disk always being first and the trash can always being last, though).

▾ No matter where you are or what is selected, if you hold the Command key down while you move an icon or group of icons, they will jump neatly to the nearest little cubby in the underlying invisible grid.

Help Menu

System 7 provides an online **Help** feature. This is useful when you come across something you've never seen before—a strange-looking icon, for example. To get Help, press on the Help menu, (the question mark inside the balloon on the far right side of the menu bar) and choose "Show Balloons."

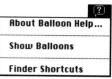

When "Show Balloons" is on, then this menu changes to "Hide Balloons."

While "Show Balloons" is on, a new balloon appears on the screen as the pointer touches an item. You don't need to press or click to see the balloon—it just appears. The text inside the balloon will explain what the item is, but not necessarily how to use it. Programs that were written especially for System 7 will have their own balloon help, so you will be able to point to an item in a program to see find out it is, like find out what a particular tool does in a drawing program.

Balloon help can be useful if you're looking for information about a specific item. And it's a novelty when you're first beginning to explore System 7. But because those balloons obscure what you're looking at and because they're so visually distracting as they pop on and off the screen, you'll probably want to go back to the Help menu and choose "Hide Balloons" as soon as you've found out about your unidentified object. The information they provide is pretty wimpy anyway.

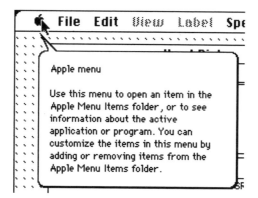

This is an example of the balloon that appears when you point to the Apple menu.

**The Application
Menu and
MultiFinder**

The tiny icon at the far right of the menu represents the **Application menu. If you have never used MultiFinder before,** please be sure to read Chapter 31, beginning on page 137. This feature is the single most visible difference with System 7, and it can be incredibly confusing if you don't know what's going on. **If you are accustomed to using MultiFinder,** this part of System 7 will be very comfortable for you.

MultiFinder allows you to have more than one application open at a time, provided you have enough memory (that's RAM, not hard disk space; see page 138). The Application menu lists the applications that are open, and you can switch back and forth between them and the Finder.

For those of you who have used MultiFinder in System 6, there are a couple of subtle changes: You must actually *choose* the application from this menu; you can no longer just click on the icon in the menu bar. Nor are your open applications listed in the Apple menu anymore. You can choose to hide all other windows except the ones you need at the moment.

CHAPTER TWENTY-SIX

SYSTEM FOLDER

System 7 has reorganized what you see in your **System Folder**—the folder that's in charge of running your Mac (see page 11). Before using System 7, you didn't have to pay much attention to what was in the System Folder as long as your Mac was working right, but with System 7 you need to know just what these new folders are and what they do because you install a lot of items (like fonts, desk accessories, sounds, printer resources, INITs, and CDEVs) simply by dragging them to your System Folder. Each item goes in a particular folder within the System Folder, but the Mac will usually take care of that for you (see "Installing Items" on page 121).

These are some of the icons and folders you will see in your System Folder:

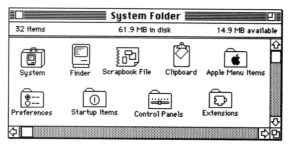

The **System file** (the file that actually runs your Macintosh) is a little different in System 7. You can actually double-click on it to see the list of fonts and sounds you have installed in your System. Each font is represented by a document icon. You can double-click on the name of a font to see a sample of what it looks like, or double-click on the name of a sound to hear it.

This is what you will see when you open the System file (double-click on it) and then double-click on a font name.

System Folder

System Folder

The Blessed System Folder

The System File

System

The System file that actually runs the show. It must stay in the System Folder.

The Clipboard and the Scrapbook

Clipboard

Scrapbook File

The Clipboard and the Scrapbook are stored in your System Folder, just as always, although the looks of their icons have changed. See page 86 for information about the Scrapbook, and pages 46–47 for information about the Clipboard.

Control Panels

Control Panels

The **Control Panels** folder holds all your control panels (yes, there's more than one Control Panel in System 7.) These control panels let you customize your Mac, as in changing your Desktop pattern and setting the mouse speed. Because there are some new control panels in System 7 and some of the old ones have changed, there's an entire chapter devoted to them. See page 123.

Apple Menu Items Folder

Apple Menu Items

The **Apple Menu Items** folder contains the icons of every item on your Apple menu (the menu on the far left of the menu bar). You can put documents, programs, folders, desk accessories—anything you like—on your Apple menu by dragging their icons to this folder. (No more Font/DA Mover for this!)

When you double-click on a suitcase that contains desk accessories, System 7 opens the suitcase to a window, and each accessory has its own icon. You can double-click the icon of any desk accessory to open and use it, whether it is stored in the Apple Menu Items folder or not. See page 113 for details.

Startup Items Folder

Startup Items

Any documents or programs that you store in the **Startup Items** folder will automatically open each time you start your Mac. This is very handy, for instance, if you are busy for weeks on the same project—every time you turn on your computer, you can have your project open automatically for you. Or you can put your hard disk icon in here and then every time you turn on your Mac your hard disk window will open. It's best to put *aliases* into this folder, rather than the originals (see page 127).

The **Extensions** folder holds certain System-related icons that help run your Mac or your peripheral equipment. Your printer icons (page 56) are stored in this folder. If you have a PostScript printer, you should store your printer font icons here (page 68). Most INITs (see page 148) should be stored in the Extensions folder. This folder also contains utilities that let you share files on a network. See "Installing Items," below.

Extensions Folder

Extensions

The **Preferences** folder contains files that have settings about how your programs think you want them to work. You can't open the icons in this folder because they're created by your programs. Don't worry about putting anything in here—the program and System 7 will take care of that.

Preferences Folder

Preferences

When you're ready to add, or **install,** something to your Mac's *System,* like a font or a desk accessory or a new control panel device (CDEV; see page 144) or an INIT (see page 148), just drag its icon to your System Folder. The Mac will ask if it's OK to put the item in the appropriate folder. Yes, it's OK. Let the Mac figure out which folder it belongs in so you don't have to.

Installing Items into the System Folder

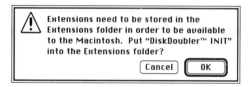

⚠ Extensions need to be stored in the Extensions folder in order to be available to the Macintosh. Put "DiskDoubler™ INIT" into the Extensions folder?

[Cancel] [OK]

Important Note: When installing items, drag the new item to the closed folder icon (even if it's gray) of your System Folder, not to the *open window* of the System Folder.

System Folder

Drag the icon to the closed
System Folder.

System

Do not drag the icon
to the **System file!**
(except fonts)

CHAPTER TWENTY-SEVEN

CONTROL PANELS

In System 7 you have separate **control panels** that let you customize the look and feel of your Mac. They're on your Apple menu; just choose Control Panels and you'll see icons for them all. Double-click each separate icon to open each control panel. You can also access each one directly from the System Folder: double-click on the "Control Panels" folder.

The control panel called **General Controls** is a little different than in earlier System versions (see page 81) in that the Keyboard, Sound, and Mouse settings are on control panels of their own now. Everything else that is left in this panel works the same as shown on pages 81–82.

The **Views** control panel lets you customize the look of your Desktop (Finder) windows. You can pick a different font and a different size instead of the standard 9-point Geneva. (Nearsighted? Try a bigger size.) As soon as you make a choice, the Mac immediately shows you how it looks. You can also choose whether you want your icons lined up in rows or staggered.

Control Panels

Control Panels

General Controls

General Controls

Views

Views

To see both lines of the information bar (as in the example in the right column), click this checkbox.

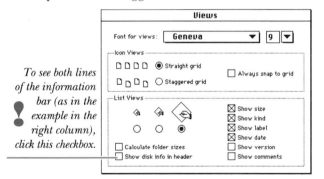

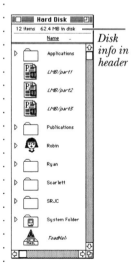

Disk info in header

The bottom portion of the Views control panel lets you choose the information to display when you're viewing a window by one of the lists (Name, Size, Kind, etc.). It also lets you choose how big you want the icons to be when you are in a list view. That is, now you can choose to view a window as a list of alphabetized names, yet still have each item's icon attached, as shown on the right. I did this by clicking on the button for the largest icon, as shown above.

This is great—I can have files listed alphabetically by name, yet still see their individual icons.

Labels

Labels

The **Labels** control panel is where you set up your labeling system (see pages 114–115 for details). Just type whatever you want as a name for each label. If you've got a color monitor, you can choose different colors for each label, too.

Once you've set up labels here, they immediately appear on the Label menu. Once you have applied labels to files, you can search for them, and you can view a window "by Label."

To **apply a label,** simply select the icon or group of icons and choose the label from the menu.

Sound

Sound

Use the **Sound** control panel to determine what noise you want to hear instead of the beep. System 7 has some new sounds in its repertoire. Click on the name of a sound to hear it. The last one you choose before you close the control panel is the sound the Mac will use when you need to be beeped.

Startup Disk

Startup Disk

If you have more than one hard disk attached to your Mac, use the **Startup Disk** control panel to determine which hard disk to use to start your computer.

Color

Color

The **Color** control panel only works, of course, if you have a color monitor. You can choose a color for high-lighted text, and you can choose another color to display your Finder window borders. Use the Labels control panel to change the color of your icons (see pages 114–115).

The **Monitors** control panel lets you choose how many of the available shades of gray or colors your screen will display. It also lets you determine which monitor should function as your main monitor, if you have more than one.

Monitor

Monitors

Mouse and **Keyboard** haven't changed in System 7; they're just separate control panels now. See pages 82–83 for hints about how you might like to set them.

Easy Access lets you use the keys on the numeric keypad to move the cursor, instead of using the mouse. It's designed for people who have problems with two-handed typing or with using a mouse. It also comes in very handy in programs where you want to nudge an object just a pixel or two.

Mouse, Keyboard, and Easy Access

Mouse   Keyboard

Easy Access

This world **map** lets you see what time it is anywhere in the world and shows you the distance between cities. To find a city, just type its name in the box and then click Find. You can add your own city to the map, too.

Map

Map

Use the **Memory** control panel to set a disk cache for your Mac. A disk cache is a part of the memory your Mac uses to hold information about the most recent things it's done on your disk, like going out and getting files and saving them. The Mac will set itself to whatever it thinks is right, depending on how much memory is available.

You can also use this Memory control panel to turn on virtual memory and 32-bit addressing if you have a "big" Mac like an LC, IIci, IIsi, or IIfx.

Memory

Memory

Networking Control Panels

System 7 has several built-in networking features, and there are three control panels that let you change those settings:

Sharing Setup

Sharing Setup lets you set your user name, choose a password for yourself, and turn on your Mac's ability to share files over the network.

Users & Groups

Users & Groups lets you restrict access to your computer to specific people or lets everybody see what you've been working on.

File Sharing Monitor

File Sharing Monitor shows you what's being shared and lets you know just who's looking in your folders.

Portable

Portable

The **Portable** control panel is of use only if you have a Mac Portable. In fact, you can't even open it if you have any other type of Mac. This control panel lets you change settings for things like memory, the screen, and your modem.

CHAPTER TWENTY-EIGHT

ALIASES

Aliases are one of the greatest features in System 7. An alias is a duplicate *icon* (not a duplicate *file*) that *represents* the real thing. Once you create an alias, you can put that alias icon wherever it's easiest for you to use.

Some applications have to be in the same folder as their supplemental files, like dictionaries or preferences, to open or to function properly. When you double-click on an alias, the Mac actually goes to the *original* file and opens the original. Having an alias hanging out on your Desktop just gives you a quick path to the original file.

Say you have a program you use frequently—your word processing program, for instance. You can make an alias of MacWrite or WriteNow or What-Have-You and put it just about anywhere. How about in your Apple menu? No problem. Out on your Desktop? Sure.

Store an alias of your hard disk icon inside the "Startup Items" folder within the System Folder. Then whenever you turn on your Mac, the window to your hard disk will automatically open. Or put an alias of the document you are always working on into the folder so you instantly open to it. Leave an alias of the Chooser on your Desktop if you have to change printers often. Leave an alias of the "Apple Menu Items" folder open on the Desktop also, so you can double-click to access any desk accessory without having to go into the menu. And since you can make almost any number of aliases of any one thing, you can store aliases of your word processing program in folders all over your hard disk so you can locate it quickly, no matter where you are or what you're doing.

You can make aliases of programs, documents, desk accessories, disks, folders, control panels, etc. Aliases open up a whole new way of organizing your filing system; anything you want to use can be only one click away from wherever you are.

Aliases

AOL Mail

This alias sits on my Desktop so I can quickly pop in to check my mail.

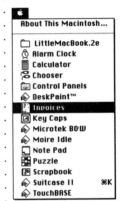

This Apple menu has an alias of the PageMaker document I use for invoices; the original is nested deep within folders. There is also an alias of the folder for this book. I put a blank space before its name so it would appear first in the list.

Making Aliases

Word alias

Making an alias is really easy.

▾ Select the item you want to make an alias of
(click once on it).

▾ From the Edit menu, choose "Make Alias."

▾ The new alias icon will look the same and will be
named the same, with the word *alias* added. An
alias name is in italic so you can always recognize
the file as an alias.

▾ Just drag the icon to wherever you want to keep it.
Rename it if you like. The new file does not have
to have the word "alias" in its name.

▾ To put the alias in your Apple menu, drag the
alias icon to the "Apple Menu Items" folder in
your System Folder.

Fine Points

Making aliases is easy, but there are a couple of fine
points you should understand.

▾ An alias isn't really a *duplicate* of anything but the
icon; it's just a *representation* of the real thing. If you
double-click on an *alias* of Word, you'll start your
original Word program running, even if the original
Word is stored in a completely different folder.

▾ If you delete an alias of something, you don't delete
the original: that's still stored on your hard disk. So
you can keep on revising your filing system as your
needs change. Don't want that alias of MacWrite
cluttering up your MacDraw folder any more? Fine;
throw it away. The original MacWrite is still where
you left it.

▾ You can move an alias and even rename an alias.
The Mac will still be able to find the original and
open it whenever you double-click on the alias.

• If you put an item into an *alias* of a folder, the item
actually gets put into the *original* folder.

▾ Even if you move or rename the *original* file, the
Mac can still find it.

▾ If you eliminate the *original* file, the Mac does not
automatically eliminate any of the representational
aliases you created.

Here are other ideas for using aliases.

▾ If you have a document you use frequently, put an alias of it in the Apple menu: just open your System Folder and drag the alias into the "Apple Menu Items" folder.

▾ If you have a program or a document that you want to open immediately whenever you turn on your Mac, put an alias of it in your "Startup Items" folder, found in the System Folder.

▾ Put aliases of folders you use often into your Apple menu, or leave aliases neatly organized directly on your Desktop.

▾ Put an alias of a Control Panel that you use over and over again out on your Desktop or in your Apple menu.

▾ Use aliases to store documents in two or three places at once. For instance, you may want to keep budget reports in folders organized by months, as well as in folders organized by projects.

▾ Use aliases to find files that you keep stored on floppy disks. Make an alias of an original file; *the original file must be on the floppy already.* Drag a copy of the alias from the floppy to your hard disk (see page 37 if you need help making copies). When you double-click on the alias on your hard disk, you will get a dialog box asking for the floppy disk that contains the original file (of course, you have to label the floppy so *you* can find it). Since aliases only take up about 2K, you can keep a folder of all those files you use only occasionally but do need to keep track of.

▾ Some of the more advanced uses for aliases aren't apparent unless you're on a network. For example, you can make an alias of your file server so you can connect to it quickly. And you can make an alias of your hard disk, copy it onto a floppy (since the alias is only about 2K), and take it to somebody elses's computer on the network. Then you can quickly connect back to your own computer just by clicking on the alias on the other computer. The concept of this "office-on-a-disk" is another place where you can begin to get a glimpse of the power of System 7.

**Finding the
Original File**

If you need to find the original file belonging to an alias,
follow these steps:

▾ Click once on the alias.

▾ From the File menu, choose "Get Info," or press
Command I.

▾ The Get Info dialog box tells you where the original
is located.

▾ If you want to have Mac go get it and bring it to you,
click the button "Find Original." The window the
original is stored in will be displayed and the icon
will be highlighted.

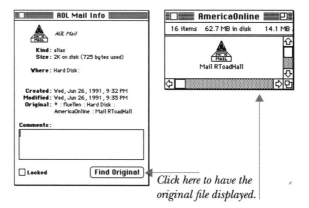

*Click here to have the
original file displayed.*

▾ If you double-click on an alias which has its original
stored on a floppy disk (see previous page), you will
get a message telling you which disk to insert.

CHAPTER TWENTY-NINE

FIND FILE

Remember Find File (page 83)? He's the little guy in the Apple menu who finds things for you. Well, in System 7 he's in the File menu as the "Find..." command with some impressive new powers.

You can find any file if you know any of this information about it:

▾ A few characters in the file's name, or what characters start or end its name.

▾ Any of the words that may be in the file's Get Info comment box (see page 31).

▾ The date you last changed the file, or when you created it.

▾ What label you assigned to it.

▾ What kind of file it is (an application, a folder, an alias, etc.).

▾ The version number.

▾ Whether it's locked or not.

▾ Whether its size is greater than or less than so many kilobytes.

Choose "Find..." from the File menu (or press Command F). You'll see this dialog box:

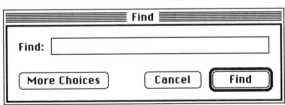

If you know the name or even part of the name of the file you're looking for, just type the characters in the Find box (it doesn't matter whether you use capital letters or lowercase letters). When you click OK, Find File will search for the first occurrence of the string of characters you typed. When a matching file is found, its window will open and the file will be highlighted. If no matching file is found, you'll hear a beep.

**Good Ol'
Mr. Find File**

Simple Finding

If the file he found isn't exactly the one you want, look for the next occurrence of that string of characters by choosing "Find Again" from the File menu (or press Command G). Keep pressing Command G until you find what you're looking for.

More Complex Finding

Instead of searching for something one file at a time, click the button "More Choices" to bring up a really sophisticated Find utility.

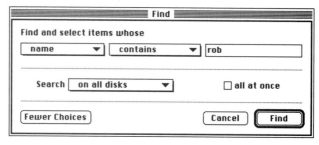

all at once

Notice the "all at once" checkbox? If you check it, Find File will find and display, simultaneously, every occurrence of whatever you've specified so that you can see all the matching files at the same time, without searching individually for each one. He does this by alphabetizing the view in your hard disk window (if that's where you searched) by name, and then expanding the appropriate folders. If you scroll down the list, you will see that every matching file is highlighted.

If Find File has expanded a lot of your folders (see page 109 for info on expanded and compressed folders) and you want them all compressed again, simply change the view to "by Icon" and then change it back to the list you prefer. All the folders will be compressed.

You can also choose where you want him to search. See the downward-pointing arrow in the label next to "Search"? Normally Find File will search all your disks, even inserted floppies. But you can press on the arrowhead to get the pop-up menu of places to search—just the Desktop, just your hard disk, just a floppy disk, just the active window, or just the folders you've selected. Narrowing your search like this can save a lot of time.

Restricting Searches

You'll notice there are also downward-pointing arrowheads next to "name" and "contains." These pop-up menus hold lots more choices. As you select different options in the first pop-up menu, the options available in the other two pop-up menus change. Try it and see.

You can get back to the simple Find box by clicking the button "Fewer Choices."

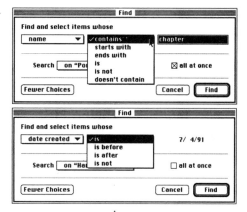

In a **search within a search** you can look for items that meet one set of criteria. Then search just those selected files for the next set of criteria. For example, suppose you have a lot of files that have "Chapter" in their names, but you only want to locate the chapters you wrote after August 16, 1991. Here's how to do that.

Search Within a Search

▾ First, search "all at once" for all files whose "name" "contains" the word chapter. Find File will find and highlight all the matching files.

Don't deselect the files! (Don't click anywhere.)

▾ From the "Search" pop-up menu, choose "the selected items."

▾ Change the search criteria to "date created" and "is after."

▾ When you choose "date created," today's date will be shown. To change the date to August 16, click once on the part of the date you wish to change, then click on the little arrows.

—continued

▾ Click the "Find" button, or hit the Return key. Find File will display only those files that have the word "Chapter" in their names that were created after August 16, 1991. It's too cool.

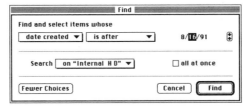

Other Search Ideas

Don't limit yourself to using "Find…" only when you are looking for a particular file. This feature can also be a lot of help if you're reorganizing your filing system. For instance, you can search by "date created" to see which of your files are outdated. Or if you're making backups, you can first search by "date modified" to see which files you haven't backed up since the last time.

This is just the tip of the proverbial iceberg of System 7's Find powers.

CHAPTER THIRTY

TRUETYPE FONTS

System 7 has a different kind of font format called **TrueType.** TrueType fonts look nice and smooth on the screen in any point size. You don't have to have a PostScript printer to take advantage of them; they work with all kinds of printers, even ImageWriters and ink-jet printers.

TrueType fonts are called **scalable fonts** because they're mathematically scalable to any size, thus you only need to have one size installed in your System to enable the Mac to create any size you need. Since TrueType fonts don't take up a lot of room, it's easier to store lots more fonts on your disk. (You'll also hear TrueType fonts being called **outline fonts.** Don't confuse that with outline style, see page 68.)

With TrueType fonts, you don't have to worry about city-named fonts vs. non–city-named fonts. You can use all TrueType fonts, no matter what their name, on any printer that will work with your Mac.

How can you tell a TrueType font from any other kind? Look at its icon, either on the floppy disk it arrived on or in the System file within the System Folder. TrueType font icons look like the one shown here, with varying letter sizes to indicate that you can use them in any size you like.

You can also tell TrueType fonts when you are inside an application: Select a font and check out the size menu. If all the sizes are in outline style, as shown to the right, then the font is TrueType.

The TrueType fonts that come with System 7 will be installed automatically when you run the Installer. If you buy any more TrueType fonts later (several vendors are making them), you'll be glad to hear that they're really easy to install. Just drag their icons into your System Folder. If you have a lot of fonts and use a utility like Suitcase II, just drag the font icons into a suitcase icon; the suitcase will accept them just as if it were a folder.

TrueType

Scalable Fonts

City-Named Fonts

How Can You Tell If It's TrueType?

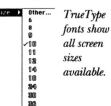

TrueType fonts show all screen sizes available.

Installing TrueType Fonts

Mixing Sixes and Sevens

The fonts you have been using with System 6 will work fine with System 7, too. You can even mix them in the same document, and everything will print just fine. The Mac will figure it all out. Just don't use the same-named font from two different vendors; that is, if you are using TrueType Times, don't keep an Adobe Times in your font list also.

Installing Other Fonts

System Folder

A closed System Folder.

LinoCaxton

A font suitcase icon.

Caxton Light 10   Caxton Light 12

Font document icons; these represent the bitmapped screen font.

CaxtoLig

An Adobe printer font icon to match the bitmapped screen font; this is what the printer needs to print the text (these icons look different from different vendors).

To install a new **non-**TrueType font to your System:

▾ Make sure your System Folder is closed, as shown.

▾ Double-click on the font suitcase icon. In earlier System versions this double-click will take you to the Font/DA Mover. In System 7, though, you will see a document icon for each font.

▾ Drag the icons of the font sizes you want to use to your System Folder. If you are using Adobe Type Manager, install just the 10-point and 12-point icons. The Mac will ask if you want it to put the items where they belong (in the System file). Yes, you do. Then close that font window.

(If you typically store your fonts in suitcases, drag the icons right to the suitcase and store the suitcase where you always have. You do not need to go through the Font/DA Mover.)

▾ If the font you are installing is a PostScript font (also known as an *outline font,* or a *Type 1* font), it comes in two parts: the bitmapped part that you just installed, and the printer font (see page 68). You must put the printer portion of the font into the closed System Folder as well (not the System *file*). Drag the icon to the System Folder; the Mac will ask if you want it to put the item in the proper folder (in the Extensions folder). Yes, you do.

(If you typically store your fonts in suitcases and use a font management utility, you still need to store the printer fonts in the same folder as the suitcase.)

TrueType fonts do not have separate icons for each size; all the sizes are rolled into the one icon. TrueType fonts do not have separate printer font icons.

CHAPTER THIRTY-ONE

MULTIFINDER

If you have been accustomed to working in **MultiFinder** in previous system versions, you can skip this chapter because it works essentially the same in System 7. If you've never used MultiFinder, this is probably the most important chapter for you to read.

MultiFinder allows you to have several applications open at the same time, as well as having access to your Desktop at all times. These are typical scenarios:

> You open MacWrite II to write a letter to the Brownie troop parents. When you decide to save the letter, you realize you forgot to make a folder in which to save this document and all the related files. So you just pop back to the Finder (Desktop), make a folder on your hard disk, and pop back into MacWrite. You didn't have to quit MacWrite to do that.

> While writing the Brownie letter, you decide to spice it up with a cute graphic. So you pop back to the Desktop, open SuperPaint, create the graphic, and pop right back to MacWrite to drop in the graphic.

> Or say you're in PageMaker and you want to make a table in the Table Editor. You can open the Table Editor, create and export the table, then drop it into PageMaker. You print it up and you notice it needs changes. Since the Table Editor is still open, you can pop right over there, fix the table, and then update the changes in PageMaker. You never had to quit one program to open the other.

> Maybe you're done with the Brownie troop letter and you want to finish that letter to Aunt Ethel. You forget where you left the letter. Find File (page 131) will get it for you, but Find File is no longer on the Apple menu *(darn it; I wish they hadn't done that)*. So you pop back to the Finder (Desktop), use Find File to dig up the letter, double-click on it, and the letter opens, taking you back to MacWrite.

Now this all seems great. It is great. Except for one thing: you have to be conscious. You have to actually *understand* what MultiFinder is doing and what you are doing.

Working in MultiFinder

**RAM
Random Access
Memory**

In order to understand how to work with MultiFinder efficiently, you need to understand RAM (Random Access Memory). Rather than send you back to page 51 to read about RAM, I'm going to repeat myself.

You have a hard disk in or next to your computer (you have to have a hard disk to run MultiFinder). Your hard disk is permanent storage space. Perhaps you have a 30 meg hard disk, or 80 meg, or 160 meg. All that storage space is permanent; *it is not considered memory.* I often hear people mistakenly calling their hard disk *memory.* It isn't. Your hard disk is like your filing cabinet; you store your applications there, your documents, your tools.

You also have a certain amount of *memory* (RAM) installed in your computer, typically from one to four megs. RAM is a *temporary* storage place. It is where all your work hangs out until you Save it onto the hard disk. When the power goes off or there is a System failure, everything in RAM disappears (that's why when you crash, you lose what you didn't Save to disk).

When you open an application, the Mac *puts a copy of the application into RAM.* It does this because RAM is much more accessible; it is much faster for the Mac to go into RAM and get work done then to keep going back to the hard disk. When you *quit* that application, Mac gets rid of the copy in memory. When you open another application, a copy of that one goes into RAM.

It is easy for RAM to get full. If it gets too full, you will crash; the Mac just checks out—says, "Oops, I've had it. I'm gone," and you get the very disturbing bomb.

**MultiFinder
and RAM**

System 7 works exclusively in MultiFinder—you can't turn it off as you can in previous System versions. While working in MultiFinder, *you can always see the Desktop,* no matter what application you are in. You can always see the trash can and your hard disk icon (although occasionally a document window may be in front of them).

This is a typical scenario: You work on a document for a while. Perhaps the document window covers up the Desktop, but when you *close* the document, it *appears* that the application has gone away and that you are back at your Desktop because you see the trash can. So you open another application. After a while you close that one.

When you try to open another application, the Mac tells you that you can't; there's not enough memory. You get confused; how can there not be enough memory? Here you are at your Desktop with nothing open. And that's the confusing thing—*you can have several applications open at once and never know it.*

Or this may happen: You're working in an application. Suddenly your menu changes—here you are in MacWrite but there's no Font menu. Or perhaps you want to Shut Down but there is no Special menu.

When working in MultiFinder, *you must constantly be conscious of your menu bar.* The menu bar is your only visual clue as to what is going on. It gives you two major indications:

▾ If you see the word "Special" in your menu bar, you are at the Finder (Desktop). If you don't see the word "Special," then you are in some sort of application. Look at the actual words in the menu bar. If all you see are "File" and "Edit," you are probably looking at a Desk Accessory (page 79). If you see "Font," you are probably in your word processor.

The point here is that you need to keep an eye on your menu bar. Once you are aware that you can bounce back and forth between applications, it is easy to find out exactly where you are (read on).

▾ In the far right corner of the menu bar is a little icon. That icon tells you which application is *active* (which one you are working in at the moment).

In the column to the right are some of the icons you may see in that corner. (If you are using System 6, you can *click* on that icon to bounce into any other open application.)

In System 7, that icon in the upper right is called the **Application menu.** If you *press* on the icon, you get a menu similar to the one shown in the right column. The bottom portion of the menu lists all the applications you have opened, as well as the Finder (Desktop). (In System 6, this list is under the Apple menu.) In the example to the right, the checkmark indicates that DeskPaint is the active application. If you choose "Finder," The Finder will become active and you will see Special in the menu bar, *but you will still see the DeskPaint window!*

Watch the Menu Bar!

When you are really at the Finder, this is the icon you will see.

When you use a Desk Accessory, you will see its icon in the corner.

This is the MacWrite II icon. When you are working in MacWrite, this icon will appear in the upper right corner.

The Application Menu

Now, that's a very conscious choice, selecting the application from the menu. It is also possible to accidentally or (preferably) consciously simply click on any open window to bounce into that application. For instance, if you are at the Finder and you want to work in DeskPaint again, you can simply click on the DeskPaint window that you see; this will make DeskPaint active and its menu will appear. *You will still see all the windows and the icons that are on the Finder* (that's what gets confusing).

Hiding the Other Windows

Since it is a well-known fact that all these open windows from the different applications can cause confusion, the Mac offers an attempt at a solution. In the Application menu you can choose to **hide the other windows.** For instance, if you are working in DeskPaint and you don't want all your Finder windows to confuse you, you can choose "Hide Others." *This does not hide the icons, like the trash can or hard disk icons, so you still see what appears to be the Desktop.* Stay conscious.

When you are in one application and want to pop into another, it is nice to hide the window you are leaving so you don't see it all over the screen. A shortcut for this is to hold down the Option key when you choose another application from the menu.

"Not enough memory" messages

At some point you will probably see a message like one of these (I see these all the time because I only have four megs of RAM):

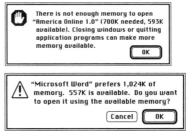

When you do, check the Application menu to see if you forgot to *quit* from an application. Too often we just *close* the current document (window), or bounce into another application or back to the Finder, and don't realize we left the first application still open. If you see an application listed that you no longer need open, choose it. Then from its File menu, choose "Quit."

PART III

JARGON
IMPRESS YOUR FRIENDS

The computer world is full of all kinds of abstruse jargon and many of us are too embarrassed to ask what the unfamiliar terms mean. And then when somebody tells us what they mean, half the time it still doesn't make sense but we pretend it does. For years I pretended I knew what a SIMM was. I've made a list of the most common terms you may hear so you can look them up in the privacy of your own room. This isn't a complete list, but it should take care of most needs. If you don't see what you want here, also look in the index. If it's not listed here or in the index, you probably don't need to know that word anyway. An italicized word within the definition means it is also in the list.

Adobe Type Manager (ATM) is a *software* program that smooths outs the edges of type on the screen. Since *QuickDraw* printers (ImageWriters, HP DeskWriters, Apple StyleWriters, fax modems, etc.) print what they see on the screen, if the type looks good on the screen it will look good in print.

Adobe Type Manager

An **accelerator board** is a *card* you can buy. You install it or have installed into your Mac. It makes the computer work faster.

accelerator board

An **alert box** is a message that appears on the screen to warn you of some imminent disaster.

alert box

AppleTalk is how your Mac talks to your LaserWriter or to other Macs or to other sorts of machines (provided they are hooked together with cables).

AppleTalk

ASCII (pronounced *askee*) stands for American Standard Code for Information Interchange. It's a standard code that almost all computers can read that enables them all to understand how to create numbers and letters, even though they use different programs. For instance, if you are working in FullWrite and you need to send the file to someone else, but they use MacWrite II, you can save the document as an ASCII file (which is the same as *text-only*) and their MacWrite II will be able to open the file.

ASCII

askee See *ASCII.*

ATM See *Adobe Type Manager.*

baud rate When you use a *modem* to send information from one computer to another, the information goes through the phone lines at a certain rate of *bits* per second. This bits-per-second rate is also called the **baud rate.** Modems most typically send at 1200, 2400, or 9600 baud.

BBS **BBS** stands for Bulletin Board Service, which is a service usually set up by organizations or clubs to provide or exchange information. You access the BBS through your *modem.* You call up the number for the BBS, and on your screen you see the computer equivalent of a bulletin board. You can post messages, ask questions, answer questions, make new friends.

beta When a piece of *software* or *hardware* is in the testing stage, it is said to be in **beta.** Usually beta versions are sent out to people to test (called beta testers) who report back the things that are wrong or buggy or that need improvement.

bit **Bit** is short for "binary digit." It's the smallest unit of information that the computer works with; it's kind of like an on/off electronic pulse. See page 7.

bitmapped When an image or text is *bitmapped,* that means it is built out of the dots on the screen. Bitmapped graphics can be edited dot by dot. They are the simplest form of imagery on the computer.

  Other kinds of graphics, *EPS,* for instance, or *PostScript* fonts, have two parts to them: They have a screen representation that is bitmapped so the computer can read and produce it on the screen. Then they also have a *PostScript,* or *outline* version of the same image that is *not* bitmapped; this is the part that the printer reads to produce it on paper.

bomb I don't think it's nice of them to use a **bomb** metaphor when the System *crashes.* It's very disturbing. It lays a guilt trip on us, too; we always think it's our fault.

boot To **boot** or **boot up** means to turn on your computer or other *hardware* or to open the *software* application. See page 11.

The B word. If a piece of *software* or *hardware* has something wrong with it, making it act weird, it is said to have a **bug** or to be **buggy.** That's something *beta* testers do—they try to find and report the bugs in new products so the bugs get exterminated before we pay lots of money for the products. The term actually comes down to us from the real live crawling and flying bugs that used to get into those giant-sized computers and wreak havoc, particularly one at Harvard in 1945.

bug

See *BBS*.

bulletin board

A **bus** is a piece of hardware that attaches to the back of the Mac and lets you plug more things into it.

bus

A **byte** is eight *bits* strung together to make a message that the computer can interpret. See page 7.

byte

CAD stands for Computer Aided Design. It actually has nothing to do with the sort of desktop publishing design projects that most of us think of—it is referring to engineering and architectural tasks.

CAD

A **card** is a piece of plastic with *chips* attached to it that you put inside the computer box. You can get video cards and accelerator cards and clock cards and printer cards or whole computers on a card. Some of them you can just order through the mail and then open the computer and stick 'em in, which I find to be a very frightening experience.

card

A **chip** is that truly amazing and remarkably tiny piece of silicon that has an entire integrated electronic circuit embedded in its surface. Chips are what make the computer. Chips are the computer. A tiny chip is one of the biggest pieces of human-made magic on earth.

chip

CD-ROM stands for Compact Disk, Read-Only Memory. A CD-ROM actually looks just like the CDs we play music with. You can get a CD-ROM player for your Mac that will read these disks. There are disks with the entire works of Shakespeare, with dictionaries, with history, with images of the works in the Louvre, etc. etc. etc. You can only read from them, you cannot store information onto them.

CD-ROM

CDEV   A **CDEV** is a control panel device. It's a little program (or *utility*) that usually makes life easier for you, like a screen saver. You can control some of their functions through the Control Panel. CDEVs are similar to *INITs* in that you just stick them in the System Folder and they work.

CPU   The **CPU** is the Central Processing Unit. It is the one tiny little *chip* in the Macintosh, often called the microprocessor, that runs the show. Powerful magic. Sometimes people refer to the circuit board it lives on as the CPU.

crash   There's probably not much question about what a **crash** is. The first time it happens to you, you say, "Oh. This must be a crash. I get it now." When you see the *bomb* on the screen or when the screen freezes or when the Mac just decides to check out, that is a crash. The only thing you can do at that point is turn the computer off. Wait several minutes before you turn it back on again. Sometimes you may have a clue as to why it crashed (see page 95); sometimes you just have to accept the fact that you will never know why. Yes, everything you did not Save to your disk is gone.

database   A **database** document is like a giant collection of 3 x 5 cards. Since they're on the computer, though, a click of a button can alphabetize those "cards," select just the names you want to invite to your party, tell you who owes how much money, etc. The term "database" can refer either to the software package you create in, or to the document itself. A database is one of the most useful tools on the Mac, and it actually is an incredible amount of fun. If you've never used one before, read Guy Kawasaki's little book, *Database 101*. Everybody needs a database.

Desktop   **Desktop** refers to what you see on the screen when you turn on the Mac. See Chapter 3, page 13.

dialog box   I use the term **dialog box** loosely in this book to avoid confusing you. I refer to any of the messages you get on the screen that tell you something or ask you something as dialog boxes. Technically, some are dialog boxes and some are alert boxes and some are actually windows and there are probably a few others, but few people will argue and all will understand if you just call them all dialog boxes.

This little creature is the **Dogcow.** His name is Clarus. He says *Moof!* Sometimes he says !fooM.

Dogcow

A **dot matrix printer** is a printer that uses coarse dots to create the text and graphics on the page, like the ImageWriter.

dot matrix printer

Dots per inch is how the *resolution* of a screen, a printer, or a scanner is measured. For instance, the standard Mac screen is 72 dots per inch. This means there are 72 rows of dots in one inch. The ImageWriter II prints at 144 dots per inch. A LaserWriter prints at 300 dots per inch. The higher the number of dots per inch, the smoother the image.

dots per inch

Download means to send information from one source, like your computer, to another source, like another computer through a *modem.* Also, certain fonts must be downloaded, or sent to, your printer before they can be printed.

download

See *dots per inch.*

dpi

The **drive** is the part of the computer that takes the disks and spins them to make them work. There are floppy disk drives, the ones with the little slots where you insert a floppy disk. There are hard disk drives that are sealed inside the computer or inside the box they come in. There are removable cartridge hard disk drives that have a large slot in which to insert a cartridge hard disk.

drive

A **driver** is a piece of *software* that tells the Mac how to communicate with or operate another piece of hardware, most commonly a printer. Your System Folder has a printer driver in it. If it doesn't, you can't print.

driver

LaserWriter

The Laser Writer printer driver in System 7.

E-mail refers to the electronic mail that you can send or receive directly on your computer. Yes, it actually means people can write you letters and send them to your computer. You can turn on your Mac and go pick up your mail. Many a love affair has begun through e-mail. I know. It's really fun, too. And useful, of course. You do need to have a *modem* or be on a *network* to send or receive e-mail.

e-mail

EPS, EPSF **EPS** or **EPSF** stands for Encapsulated PostScript File. This is a graphic *file format.* Graphics that are saved as EPS are made of two parts. One part is a simple *bitmapped* image that the **computer** reads and displays on the screen. The other part is a complex *PostScript* code that the **printer** reads (if the printer reads *PostScript*). EPS files are called "device independent" or "resolution independent." This means they will print at whatever resolution the printer happens to be. The same graphic will print at 75 *dpi* on the ImageWriter II, at 300 dpi on a LaserWriter, at 1240 or 2400 dpi on Linotronics.

file format A **file format** simply means the particular structure that a document (graphics, text, spreadsheet, etc.) is saved in. For instance, in text there are file formats like *ASCII* (text-only) or RTF, in addition to the standard file format for your particular word processor, such as MacWrite II. In graphics there are file formats like *EPS, TIFF, PICT,* or MacPaint. Different programs can read different formats.

file server A **file server** is used on a *network.* Often one Mac and its hard disk are dedicated to the job of being a file server. Everybody on the network (everybody who is connected with cables to this computer) can use the software and the hard disk belonging to that Mac, rather than everyone having their own. There is also file server *software* that controls who gets to read and use what and how many people get to do it at the same time.

Finder The **Finder** is another term for the Desktop (see Chapter 3, page 13). There is also an icon in the System Folder called Finder, which controls the Desktop.

Fkey The terms **Fkey** and **function key** are used interchange-
function key ably, although there are two separate meanings.

FKey is usually referring to a mini-program, or *utility,* that can be added to your Mac (kind of like a desk accessory). The little FKey program makes things happen when you press a certain key combination, like Command Shift 7.

Function key usually refers to the 10 to 15 extra keys along the top of an extended keyboard, numbered F1 through F10 or F15, that you can program to perform certain tasks, usually with a *macro* utility.

Freeware refers to the *software* that some nice person creates and then puts out into the world at no cost to the user for the benefit of humanity and no benefit to themselves. Freeware is often available on *bulletin board services,* through *user groups,* or from friends. See also *shareware.* People who create freeware are diametrically opposite to the evil people who create *viruses.*

freeware

See *Fkey.*

function keys

A **gigabyte** (G) is a unit of measure, measuring file size or hard disk space, etc. It's very large. Technically, one gigabyte is 1024 *megabytes,* which is the same as one billion *bytes,* which is really 1,073,741,824 bytes. Impress your friends with this useful knowledge.

gigabyte G

Some Macintosh screens are **grayscale,** rather than plain ol' black-and-white. On a black-and-white screen or on printed material, gray tones are simulated by black and white dots that give the illusion of gray when seen from a slight distance. A grayscale image (a photograph, for instance, that has been *scanned* into the computer) on a black-and-white monitor (screen) is broken into dots to represent the gray values. On a grayscale monitor, though, the same image will display in actual gray values. It's very beautiful to see.

grayscale

Hard copy refers to the printed version of what you have in the computer. For instance, this book is a PageMaker file stored on a disk. I printed up hard copy for editing and for producing into the book in your hands.

hard copy

Hardware refers to the parts of the computer or of any *peripherals* you can bang on. The monitor, the external hard disk, the mouse, the keyboard, the modem, the scanner—all those things you can touch are hardware. As opposed to *software.*

hardware

The Macintosh System originally kept track of items on a disk with the Macintosh File System (MFS). Then the HFS, or Hierarchical File System was developed, which is much more efficient at keeping track of what is inside folders, and folders inside of folders. Wanna know a little-known and very useless bit of trivia? If a disk has been formatted with HFS, there is a tiny dot right here in each window (unless you are using System 7).

HFS, or hierarchical file system

INIT An **INIT** (accent on the second syllable) is a little program that does things like make extra sounds, pictures, bizarre cursors, clocks, etc. Some applications have INITs as an adjunct to the main program. INITs work only if they are stored inside your blessed System Folder; if you put them in any other folder, they don't work.

These things are called INITs because they work upon *initialization* of your computer; that is, when you start it up (they're also known as Startup Documents). When you turn your machine on, all these little INITs get loaded into RAM* and start working even before your System gets up and running. Those little icons that appear in the lower left portion of your screen as you *boot up* represent your INITs (some are also *CDEVs,* which are like INITs except that you have some control over them through the Control Panel).

INITs are a well-known source of trouble to the System. If things start acting weird after you install an INIT, take the INIT back out, restart (from the Special menu), and see if things are normal again. Never install more than one INIT at a time; rather, put one in, work on your machine a few days, then put another one in. That way you will be able to pinpoint the one that causes trouble. (For instance, I've heard of an INIT that inadvertently affects the column guides in PageMaker. Weird.)

*Read up on RAM to understand the effect of having INITs taking up space. See pages 51, 138, and 196.

initialize When you buy a new floppy disk or a hard disk, it is unformatted; that is, it is completely blank and doesn't have any of the tracks necessary in which to lay down the data you are going to give it. So you have to **initialize** it. Blank hard disks come with special software to use for initializing them. When you insert a blank floppy disk, the Mac asks if you want to initialize it (see page 8). You have to, if you want to use it.

If you re-initialize any disk, the process permanently erases anything that currently exists on that disk.

As noted in the section on INITs above, the term *initialization* is sometimes referred to as the booting up of the computer.

Kerning is the process of adjusting the fit between letters. You can only do it in certain programs, like the more expensive page layout or illustration applications.

To **launch** simply means to start or open an application.

Leading (*ledding*) is the amount of space between lines of text. It is typically measured in *points*. In page layout programs and in some word processing programs you can adjust the amount of space between the lines.

A **ligature** is a typographic nicety; it is one character that is actually two single characters combined together. For instance, when you type the letter f next to the letter i, the hook of the f bumps into the dot of the i. The ligature for f and i is one character, like so: fi. Every *PostScript* font on the Mac includes the common ligatures for fi and fl (see the chart of the last page of this book for the keystrokes). Certain other fonts, like the Adobe Expert collections, contain many more ligatures.

Lines per inch is very different than *dots per inch*. Dots per inch refers to the *resolution* of the screen, the scanner, or the printer, which can get up into the 2000 dots per inch range. The lines and curves of text appear to be perfectly smooth because the dots are so small our eyes can't separate them.

But when a graphic that is in gray tones or in color, such as photographs or gray bars, goes to the printing press or a copy machine, the tones must be broken into dots big enough to print ink or toner. The principle is the same as in dots per inch: 85 lines per inch means that in an inch there are 85 lines of dots. The more lines that fit into an inch, the smaller the dots. The smaller the dots, the higher quality the printing press must be in order to **hold** (print clearly) the dots. Copy machines and newspapers need graphics at 65 to 85 lines per inch. Low-cost presses (quick printers) need 85 to 100 lines per inch. A good press can usually print 133 lines per inch. Only very high-quality art-type books are printed higher than 133 line.

An Apple LaserWriter has a default for grayscale graphics of 53 lines per inch, which means that any gray image that comes out of the LaserWriter will have the gray values broken up into dots in lines of 53 per inch.

kern

launch

leading

ligature

fire fire
flirt flirt

lines per inch

log on, log off These terms refer to the process of checking in, or **logging on,** to a *bulletin board service* or a *network,* or to the process of checking out, **logging off.** Typically when you log on somewhere you have to have a password.

macro The term **macro** sounds very arcane and intimidating, but once you use them you get hooked, they are so cool. A macro is simply a series of steps (menu commands, mouse clicks, keystrokes, etc.) that are programmed into one key or one key combination. Once it is programmed and you press that key combination, the entire series of steps is executed at high speed.

For instance, if you're creating a database of names and addresses, you can create a macro that will type "P.O. Box " for you so you just press one key combination and that phrase will appear. Or if you regularly have to type the phrase "Robin's and Janet's Private Club for the Dissemination and Elucidation of Macintosh Magical Mysteries," make a macro for it. If at the end of each week you always gather up all the accounts entered, copy them, open another spreadsheet, drop them in, then print up a report with sums and totals and balances, create a macro for it. Anything you do repeatedly, you can lighten your life by making a macro for it.

Do-it-yourself macros are very easy to create; basically, you just say Do This, show it what to do, and the macro Does It. Some applications, like Microsoft Works, have a macro feature built right into it. Apple provides Macro-Maker with its System software (which I don't use because it interrupts Dark Castle). Ask around about them.

memory **Memory** is generally referring to RAM, which is Random Access Memory. Memory is temporary, volatile storage space, as opposed to the permanent storage space you have on a disk. You should read pages 51, 138, and 196 about RAM to get a good grasp on this important subject.

modem A **modem** is a little box that sits next to your computer. It has a cable that plugs into your Mac. It has another cord that plugs into your phone jack. With a modem hooked up, then, your computer can call any other computer that is also hooked up to a modem. You can sit at your computer and "talk" to other people who are sitting at their computers. You type a couple lines of conversation, hit the Return key, and your conversation shows up on both of your computer screens. It's really addictive. People have been known to meet and eventually marry through meeting *online* (on the screen). And many a one-night-online-stand has happened. It's a fascinating phenomenon.

But, practically speaking, an incredible amount of business goes on through the modem. You can send any file through the phone lines. If you live out in the boonies, you can send your publication out for high-level output to a service bureau hundreds of miles away; they'll just express the finished product back to you through the mail. If your magazine column is due by 12 noon on Friday, you can finish it at 11:45 and still have it in their hands across the country by noon. You can conduct research, make plane reservations, join clubs, play long-distance chess, oh the possibilities are endless.

Just so you know, the word modem is derived from the terms **mod**ulator and **dem**odulator.

Modifier keys are the ones that have no character attached to them, but that alter the behavior of another key. These are Macintosh modifier keys: Shift, Option, Command, Caps Lock, and Control (if your keyboard has it). Always when using modifier keys you press those keys down and *hold* them, and then just *tap* the character key that it modifies. For instance, the keyboard shortcut for Paste is Command V. So hold down the Command key and tap the letter V. If you *hold* the letter V down, you'll end up pasting in more than one of the item.

modifier key

The term **moiré** refers to the bizarre patterns that result in photographs (or other graphic images with color or gray values), when lines of dots at one angle overlap lines of dots at another angle (see *lines per inch*). It's not easy to avoid them if you're trying to print directly from the computer output, rather than high-quality separations. How to avoid them "is beyond the scope of this book."

(I see stuff all the time telling people to pronounce this word "mwahr" or "mwah ´ray," but nobody says it like that. Maybe if you're French you do, but American mouths don't work that way. This term's been around a lot longer in printing and graphics than computer nerds realize. [Me, I'm not a nerd; I'm a nerdette.] Just pronounce it "**mor ay**," with the accent on the second syllable, and you will be perfectly acceptable.)

moiré

Moof!™ · **Moof!** is what the *Dogcow* says.

motherboard · Isn't this a nice name? It's also called a "logic board," but **motherboard** sounds so much more earthy and close to the heart. The motherboard contains the heart of the Mac. It's the board, or piece of fiberglass, that contains the most important *chips* that run the computer, including the *RAM* and the *CPU* (Central Processing Unit).

multimedia · This was the biggest buzzword in town a few years ago. Now it's become the M word, the equivalent of saying "Have a nice day." **Multimedia** refers to presentations that are created using a variety of media, such as sound, video, graphics, and text.

nested · When folders are stored inside of folders, they are said to be **nested.** Folders can be nested ad infinitum (well, about 12 layers deep in System 6; the Computer God only know how many in System 7).

network · When you connect computers together, either directly through cables or else through *modems* and phone lines, they are all on the same **network.** People on a network can share files, applications, e-mail, etc. Also see *file sharing*.

object-oriented · Some programs, like MacPaint, create everything *bitmapped,* where dots on the screen are either on or off and you can edit images dot by dot. Other programs, like MacDraw, are **object-oriented** and create images as entire objects. You can't edit the objects dot by dot; you can only change the entire object as a whole. Each object is on a separate, transparent layer, and is defined by a mathematical formula rather than bitmapped dots. Since they are not bitmapped, object-oriented graphics print much smoother, taking advantage of the resolution of the printer.

OCR · **OCR** stands for Optical Character Recognition. It's a combination of *software* and *hardware* that is able to take text on a printed page, *scan* it into the computer, and have the computer turn the text into the *characters,* not into a graphic image. That means you can take all the typed letters your lovers have sent you over the past ten years and input them into your computer *without retyping them.* This opens up incredible possibilities.

When you are talking through your computer to another computer or to an information service (see *BBS* or *modem*), you are **online.**

online

Online help is the file an application provides within itself where you can find information about the program or how to work it, without ever leaving the application or your computer. It's a manual on screen. Usually they're pretty wimpy, although they can be of use. System 7 has an online Help feature. It's pretty wimpy.

online help

When people talk about **outline** fonts, they are not talking about the outline style (gag). Fonts come in basically three varieties: bitmapped, outline, and TrueType. TrueType is discussed in Chapter 30, so we will ignore it here (it is an altogether different creature). So then:

outline font

LinoCaxton

    Bitmapped fonts are usually named after a city (Monaco, New York, etc.). They are stored in suitcase icons. They are built out of the dots on the screen. When you print a bitmapped font on any printer, regardless of the resolution, the letters are still bitmapped and lumpy.

Bitmapped fonts, whether they are city-named fonts or the screen portions of an outline font, are always stored within a suitcase icon. The icon above stores the fonts in the Caxton family: Caxton Light, Caxton Bold, Caxton Light Italic, and Caxton Bold Italic (four fonts).

    Outline fonts are made of two parts: One part is the screen font (which is exactly like a bitmapped font, stored in a suitcase, and built out of the dots on the screen; don't get confused). The screen font is what appears in your menu and is what you use to create the document. The screen font is what the **computer** reads.

    The second part of an outline font is the printer font. Each outline font needs a corresponding printer font. The printer font is written in the *PostScript* language. When you print to a PostScript printer, the printer ignores the font you see on the screen. The **printer** reads the printer font. If you are using 37-point outline type and it looks crummy on the screen, it will still print nice and smooth on a PostScript printer.

CaxtoLig

Ouline fonts must have a corresponding printer font for each member of the font family; that is, this icon above is for Caxton Light. In order to print the other three font family members, I must have the printer font for each one.

peripherals Any *hardware* that is attached to the computer is considered a **peripheral.** Modems, scanners, CD-ROM players, printers, external hard disk drives, etc., are all peripherals.

pirate In computer jargon, **pirate** is a verb that describes making a copy of commercial software without permission and without paying for it. It is essentially stealing.

pica A **pica** is the unit of measure that typesetters have used for many years to measure type and line lengths. There are six picas in one inch (one pica =.167 inch), and there are 12 *points* in each pica.

PICT A **PICT** is a graphic *file format,* generally used for *object-oriented* graphics. They don't take up much disk space, and most programs can read them. They're rather undependable, though (in fact, I hate them). If you are saving a graphic as a PICT, make sure there are no *bitmapped* graphics within it, and don't use any *downloadable* fonts. Even then, they often decide to change their appearance without warning you.

Pict

pixel A **pixel** (**pic**ture **el**ement) is the smallest dot that the Macintosh can display on the screen or that the printer can print. On a standard Mac screen, each pixel (each dot) is $\frac{1}{72}^{nd}$ of an inch (remember, the *dots per inch* is 72). On the Apple LaserWriter, each pixel is $\frac{1}{300}^{th}$ of an inch.

point A **point** is the unit of measure that typesetters have used for many years to measure the size of type and the space between the lines. It is the unit of measure on the Mac to measure type and the space between the lines. There are 72 points in one inch. There are 72 *dots per inch* on the standard Macintosh screen. That was not an accident.

    (For type aficionados: you will be interested to know that 72 points on the Mac equals exactly one inch.)

port **Port** is just another name for a plug (a socket, actually) on the back of the Mac where you plug the cords and cables in. You can't go wrong with plugging things in— there is either a picture above the port giving you a clue as to what should go in the socket, or the port is shaped in such a way that only one kind of plug will fit.

    Port also refers to rewriting software so it works on another kind of computer.

PostScript is a programming language developed by Adobe Systems that has become an industry standard. It's a language that *PostScript-compatible printers* read (as opposed to a language that your *computer* reads). It is PostScript that enables complex graphics to be printed at any resolution (whatever the resolution of the printer). Also see *PostScript printer.*

PostScript

A **PostScript printer** (or PostScript-compatible printer) is a printer that can interpret the graphics and fonts that are written in the PostScript programming language. Not all laser printers can read PostScript. Just because a printer has a high *resolution* does not mean it is PostScript. For instance, the Apple StyleWriter prints at 400 *dots per inch,* but it is not PostScript. Usually if a printer is not PostScript, it is a *QuickDraw printer.*

PostScript printer

Once you start using keyboard commands, install a few *INITs* and *CDEVs,* create a *macro* or two, and start throwing around words like *RAM* and *PostScript,* you can consider yourself a **power user.** Say the word *SIMM, motherboard,* or *CPU* in mixed company and you will really get respect.

power user

Public domain is an adjective describing any kind of work, not just computer *software,* for which the public has every right to copy and use in any way they see fit. The author has retained no rights nor liabilities. Usually cuz they're dead. Public domain software is different than software that is copyrighted to the author yet distributed publicly. See *freeware* and *shareware.*

public domain

QuickDraw is the computer code that lives in the Mac's *ROM* (read-only memory) and is used for drawing graphics on the screen and on the printer.

QuickDraw

A **QuickDraw printer** is generally almost any printer that can't read *PostScript.* If a printer cannot read Post-Script, then it has to just recreate what it sees on the screen. That's the big deal about *ATM* (Adobe Type Manager). ATM makes certain typefaces clear and relatively smooth on the screen; thus when they print to a QuickDraw printer, they are much clearer and smoother on the page.

QuickDraw printer

RAM, see pages 51, 96, and 138

read-only When a file or a disk is **read-only,** that means you can
look at and print the file or disk, but you cannot save
changes onto it. Often you think you can, because the file
lets you select and edit text, but when you go to Save it,
you won't be allowed. Locking a disk or file (page 94) will
make it read-only. *CD-ROMs* are read-only. A certain part
of the Mac's inner workings are read-only.

ReadMe You will usually see a **ReadMe** file on a disk when you get
a new software package. It's a good idea to read them
(how can you resist?) because they describe the product
and often give you the details on any last-minute changes.

redraw When you move an object across the screen, scroll,
change windows, etc., all or part of the screen has to be
redrawn. The Mac has to figure out where everything
has moved to and redraw them in their new places.

refresh rate How quickly a screen is *redrawn* is called the **refresh rate.**
Faster is better, of course.

resolution The **resolution** of a computer screen or printer is
measured in *dots per inch.* The greater the number of dots
per inch, the higher the resolution. The higher the resolution, the smoother the graphics and text will be. The
standard Mac screen has a resolution of 72 dots per inch.
The Apple LaserWriter has a resolution of 300 dots per
inch. The Apple StyleWriter has a resolution of 400 dots
per inch.

ROM The initials **ROM** stand for Read-Only Memory, which
usually refers to the System information that is built into
the *chips* inside the computer, the information that gets
the System up and running. Also see *read-only.*

RTF **RTF** is Rich Text Format, another *file format* in which
you can save text. It holds onto a little more formatting
information than does an *ASCII* file.

scan, A **scanner** is a piece of *hardware.* What it does is **scan** an
scanner image: You put a photograph or a piece of drawn art or
sometimes a three-dimensional object on the scanner.
You close the lid and push a button, the machine views
(scans) the image, and sends a copy of it to the computer.
It's sort of like making a xerox copy, but instead of
coming out the other end, the copy comes out in the

computer. (Not all scanners work like I described here; some are hand-held and you roll the little machine over the top of the image. There are also video scanners that can input live stuff.) The image to the right was scanned in.

When you scan images, the scanning software usually offers you several *file format* options. Unless you have a clear idea and a good reason as to why you would save it in any other format, always save scanned images as TIFFs. TIFFs were invented for scans.

This was a photograph. I scanned it as a grayscale TIFF at 210 dpi.

> ▾ If the image is straight black-and-white with no gray areas, save it as a line art TIFF.
>
> ▾ If the image has gray tones, such as a photograph or pencil or charcoal drawing, save it as a gray-scale or con-tone TIFF.
>
> **Halftones:** Halftones only apply to gray or color areas. A halftone breaks the gray area into dots that a printer can print (see *lines per inch*). If the image is solid black-and-white, you don't need any sort of halftone.
>
> ▾ If your scanning software can create special effect halftones that you want to use (or if your printer is not *PostScript-compatible*), save it as a halftone TIFF.
>
> ▾ If there is no special effect halftone you need, then don't bother saving it as a halftone—let the Post-Script printer halftone it on the way out. (Yes, all PostScript printers will do that; they take any gray or color image and break it into *lines per inch*. The number of lines per inch varies depending on the printer. An Apple LaserWriter halftones at 53 lines per inch; a Linotronic 300 halftones at 105 to 150 lines per inch.)

screen saver

If you leave an image on the screen for an extended period of time, it will eventually burn in and leave a permanent shadow. A **screen saver** is a little program (a *utility*) that prevents burn in by creating interesting animated effects when you are not working. Effects range from simple fireworks to moving patterns to flying toasters with wings that you can hear beating if you listen closely. Some screen savers activate automatically if the keyboard or mouse haven't been touched in a certain number of minutes (those bug me; I hate to be interrupted while I'm thinking). Others you must turn on yourself. A good one lets you choose either.

SCSI **SCSI,** pronounced *scuzzy,* stands for Small Computer Systems Interface. SCSI is a connecting system, an interface, that allows computers and their *peripheral* devices (scanners, printers, etc.) to exchange information. Those big cables with the little pins in them (usually 50 pins or 25 pins) are SCSI connectors and they plug into SCSI *ports* on the back of the Mac.

scuzzy See *SCSI.*

shareware **Shareware** is copyrighted software that somebody went to the trouble to create and then distributed through *user groups, bulletin board services,* and friends. You can try the software for free, but if you like it you should pay for it. Shareware is generally pretty cheap ($5 to $20) and you really should pay it to encourage other people to create nice things for us.

SIMM Ha. Now I know what a **SIMM** is. It's a Single Inline Memory Module. Well, that's what techies say it is. I say it is a little piece of plastic with *chips* on it. These particular chips are *memory* chips. When you want to add more memory, more *RAM,* to your computer you buy SIMMs. Then somebody installs the SIMMs into your computer.

software *Hardware* is the stuff you can knock on. **Software** is the invisible stuff, the programming, the energy coursing through the *chips* that makes the computer work. Software is in the form of *applications,* or *programs,* in the *memory* stored inside the Mac, it's on the disks, it's in the *System* that runs the machine. It's the big magic.

spooler A **spooler** is *software* (or sometimes a combination of software and *hardware*) that allows you to work on your screen while your printer is printing. Typically what happens when you print **without** a spooler is that the computer sends the pages to the printer. The computer can send the information much faster than the printer can deal with it. So the computer has to hang around and wait while the printer processes all the information. Then it sends a little more info and waits. Sends a little more and waits. Meanwhile, you are also waiting because the computer is busy and won't let you have your screen back.

But when you use a spooler, the computer sends the information to the spooler instead of to the printer. The spooler takes it all, says thank you very much, and then funnels the information to the printer. Since the computer did its job of sending off the info, you get your screen back and you can work merrily along while the spooler finishes telling the printer what to do.

Sometimes while using a spooler your screen may get interrupted for a minute here and there while the computer takes care of details. But in general, it's painless.

Spreadsheet is another one of those terms that intimidates us at first. A *database* is for making a list of items that you can then manipulate; a *spreadsheet* is generally used for number-crunching. You can do your home budget on a simple spreadsheet (I hire my teenager to do it), create invoices for your small business, project your mortgage payments, etc. etc. etc. They are so cool. It's quite a feeling of power to set one up, plug in some numbers, and watch it work. Most spreadsheets also have a method for applying borders (lines) on the page, which means it is so incredibly easy to make great, instant forms: As you widen the page, the lines get longer; if you delete a row or a column, the lines will also be deleted; as you make the point size bigger, the space between the lines gets bigger. It's terrific, even if you don't have a single number on the page.

spreadsheet

A **stack** is a document that has been created in the application **HyperCard.** HyperCard is a very interesting and provocative program that is difficult to explain in a few sentences so I'm not going to try. The biggest single difference between something created in HyperCard and something created in almost any other program is that the document, or stack, that you create in HyperCard never leaves the computer. In almost every other program you create something on the computer and then print it up and you hand out the printed piece. In HyperCard, what you create is meant to be viewed by other people directly on the computer. It works in a series of cards (hence the term *stack*, as in stack of cards). As you flip through the cards of information, you may find sounds and animation and music and interactions. It's really an exciting and addictive program to work in, but you must keep in mind that for anyone to use your final project, they have to have a Macintosh.

stack

HyperCard

The application HyperCard.

Addresses

A stack, or document, created in HyperCard.

startup volume Some people have more than one hard disk attached to their computer. Sometimes more than one of those hard disks has a System Folder (be careful! don't do that unless you know why and how to deal with two System Folders). The hard disk that is running the machine at the moment is the **startup volume.** Or you could call it the startup disk, but usually people refer to it as a volume if it is a hard disk. The startup volume *boots* the computer. The startup volume will always put its icon in the top right corner.

suitcase The term **suitcase** gets confusing because two very important, closely related, but not connected items both refer to it: *suitcase icons* and the font management program called *Suitcase II.*

FuturaFamily

Desk Accessories

Suitcase icons

Suitcase icons represent *screen fonts* or *desk accessories.* In System 6 you can't open these suitcases, really. If you double-click on a suitcase to try to see the fonts or DAs inside, you will go straight to the Font/DA Mover (see page 61). While in the Font/DA Mover you can click on the name of a font to see it displayed. [In System 7, if you double-click on a suitcase it opens up to a window with an icon for each font size and you can double-click each one to take a look at it; see page 119 and 136.]

Suitcase™ II

Icon for Suitcase II font management program

There is also a wonderful program called **Suitcase II** which helps you work more efficiently when you have a large number of fonts. It also resolves font conflicts, or identity crises, which is what happens regularly when a lot of fonts get together. If you're a font freak (meaning you like and collect them), it is absolutely indispensable to use a program like Suitcase II or Master Juggler to manage your fonts (even with System 7, no matter what they tell ya).

But the confusion occurs because people banter around the word *suitcase* referring to either the screen font icon *or* to the font management program, and a beginner doesn't see the difference yet.

system crash You'll know a **system crash**, or bomb, when you see one. Either you get a very polite yet disturbing notice on your screen with a picture of a bomb about to explode (cute, very cute), or things will just stop working. Your keys won't work, the mouse won't work. The only thing you can do is turn the computer off. See pages 195–196 for a couple of reasons why you might crash, how to avoid crashing, and what to do about it when it does happen (which it will).

TeachText is a tiny little word processing program (it only takes up 36K of disk space). Often when you get new software you will see an icon called *ReadMe*. This file has the latest info on the software, or maybe some tricks you should know about. To make sure you can read the file, since the software company has no idea what word processing program you use or even if you have one, they write the ReadMe file in TeachText, and then also send along the TeachText application on the disk so you can open ReadMe.

TeachText

TeachText

The term **telecommunications** refers to communicating over the phone lines through a *modem* as opposed to using your voice. It's even faster than overnight mail.

telecommunications

A document that is formatted (saved) as   is able to be read by almost any word processing or page layout program. It has no formatting, like font size or style or columns, etc. Text-only is synonomous with *ASCII,* so you should take a quick moment to look up that term (it's on page 141).

text-only

TIFF stands for Tagged Image File Format. It is a format used for saving or creating certain kinds of graphics. Graphics in TIFF are always *bitmapped,* but the bitmap resolution can be very high, depending on the program you are working in. TIFFs can be black-and-white line art, or they can be *grayscale* images. They were invented for *scanning,* so you might want to also read the scanning information (page 156).

TIFF

Some menu commands and keyboard shortcuts are **toggle** switches. This means if you choose it once, the command is turned on; if you choose the same command again, it is turned off. Sometimes a command that can be toggled shows up with a checkmark next to it (although a checkmark does not mean it is necessarily a toggle switch!). Sometimes a command that can be toggled changes the name of the command when you choose it (e.g., "Show Clipboard" becomes "Hide Clipboard"). See "Changing Styles Mid-Stream" on page 45.

toggle

Type 1 font
There are two* distinct formats for type, **Type 1** and *Type 3* (there really isn't a *Type 2* format). The corporation Adobe Systems, Inc., had a monopoly on Type 1 fonts; they used a secret formula to produce them and wouldn't let anybody else have the formula. So everybody else had to make Type 3 fonts.

Type 1 fonts are *PostScript,* and they are especially designed to print well at "low" resolutions (like 300 *dpi*). They print fast and clean on PostScript printers, and they can be scaled with *Adobe Type Manager (ATM)* to appear very smooth on your screen. In 1990 Adobe decided to publicize the secret formula so everyone ("everyone" meaning font manufacturers) can create Type 1 fonts.

*System 7 introduces a new font format called TrueType. If you're interested, read Chapter 30.

Type 2 font
Type 2 was a proposed font technology that never made it, so there are no Type 2 fonts.

Type 3 font
Type 3 fonts are the typefaces that are made without Adobe System's proprietary font technology. They tend to be less expensive, and they often don't print as clean and smooth, nor as fast, as *Type 1* fonts. They also tend to be more graphic in nature; that is, many Type 3 fonts are very decorative, with gray shades and elaborate fills and fancy shadows.

upgrade
When a company improves their software or hardware, that improvement is called an **upgrade.** The upgrades are indicated by the *version number;* e.g., PageMaker 4 is in its fourth major upgrade since it was invented. Minor little fix-its are noted by points *(well, that's the only word I could think of).* For instance, PageMaker is currently in version 4.01 (pronounced four point oh one). If you are a registered owner of the software, you can usually purchase an upgrade at a significantly reduced cost, and sometimes you even get the upgrade free. If your *hardware* goes through an upgrade, you just have to buy the new piece.

upload
When you use your *modem* to copy information off of another computer and put it on yours, you are *downloading* (taking it down from the other computer). When you use your modem to put information onto another computer, you are **uploading** (putting it up onto the other computer).

A **utility** is an application, generally a very small application, that has a very limited function. Utilities don't create documents; they just make things work better or add a bit of sparkle or convenience to your computer. The Font/DA Mover (Chapter 19) is a utility. *Adobe Type Manager* is a utility.

utility

When a company announces that their software is about to appear on the market and then it doesn't appear when it is supposed to, that software is considered **vaporware.** The term even gets loosely applied to books that don't appear on time, or blind dates.

vaporware

A **video card** is the *card* (the piece of plastic with *chips* attached to it) that controls the display on your screen. You can get different kinds of video cards for different kinds of monitors that allow the monitor to display different levels of *grayscale* or colors.

video card

Viruses are very interesting things. A **virus** is a program that a very intelligent, very skilled, and very evil, sick person writes. It is written to do such things as destroy the data on your computer, corrupt your System, lock you out of your own machine, eat your programs. They can wipe out an entire hard disk. Viruses travel from computer to computer through floppy disks, networks, and even modems. You don't always know you have a virus; they often have a delayed reaction time, so you use the sick program for a while until one day it eats you. It seems that a person who can write a program to do so much evil is certainly bright enough to get a real job and direct that energy into making people happy instead.

virus

   This is a virus scenario: You have a disk that is infected. You put it into your Mac. As you use an application on that disk, the virus gets into your System. You take that disk out and insert another one. The virus jumps from your System onto an application on the floppy disk. You take that disk out, go to another computer in the office and insert it. The virus jumps from that disk onto the other person's System. Ad infinitum. The WDEF virus is so contagious that simply inserting an infected disk into a computer infects the computer. It's sort of comparable to somebody with a social disease getting on a bus and everybody on the bus automatically getting the disease. Then *virus* *(continued)* everybody on the bus gets off the bus and goes into the stores and everybody in the stores gets the disease. Fortunately WDEF is not a terribly devastating virus, just very irritating. See page 92 for an easy way to get rid of this pest (System 7 is immune to WDEF and to CDEF).

How do you know when you have a virus? Things start acting funny on your computer. Windows may not function properly, printing might not work right, files may be changed, programs may be "damaged." If anything starts acting weird, you can suspect a virus. (Actually, first you should suspect any *INITs* or *CDEVs* you may have in your System folder, since they are a much more likely cause of little troubles. Take them all out and put them back in again, one at a time, over a period of a couple of days. That way you can pinpoint the offensive creature and remove it.) If you think the problem really is a virus, then get virus-protection software and disinfect your hard disk *and every single disk in your entire house and office.* And never again let anyone put a disk in your computer without checking it first.

Everyone should own virus-protection software as a normal part of computer life. The best package is one called **Disinfectant.** It has an application that will locate and kill any virus, and it comes with an *INIT* that will quietly check any disk you put in your machine. If an infected disk is inserted, Disinfectant sets off bells and whistles (literally). It is *freeware,* written by a wonderful man named John Norstad at Northwestern University. He spends time to write this program and is constantly updating it to catch new viruses. Can you believe that? He does this out of the kindness of his heart, an intrepid soul battling the forces of evil. Write him a nice thank-you letter and tell him how wonderful he is.

Disinfectant is available on several of the *bulletin board services,* from *user groups,* or from friends. You do need to be on the lookout at all times for the latest version of it, since those evil minds are constantly striving to outsmart the current virus-protection software.

Viruses have the potential to cause catastrophic damage; however, most Macintosh viruses have been held in check by virus-protection software, and with a little knowledge you can easily protect yourself and your loved ones.

See *WYSIWYG*, just below.

wizziwig

WYSIWYG stands for What You See Is What You Get, which means that what you see on the screen is what will print out on paper. If you are just beginning to use a Mac and you have never used any other computer, you may wonder what the big deal is about wysiwyg because of course that's the way it is and that's the way it should be. But it is actually a relatively new concept, and one where the Mac excels over those other machines.

WYSIWYG

These numbers designate different *chips* (designed by Motorola). These particular chips run the computers, and the higher the number the faster and more powerful the machine. For instance, the 68000 chip is the one in the older Macs, like the 128, the 512, the Plus, and the SE. The Mac II has a 68020 and runs about five times faster than the 68000. The 68030 was a big deal and was installed in the SE/30, IIx, and IIcx. And the 68040 is of course even faster and does more tricks.

68000
68020
68030
68040
etc.

Other important chips have these other numbers and do things like increase the floating point mathematics speed by about 100 times, whatever that means.

68551
68882
etc.

INDEX

Colophon

The second edition of this book was produced on a Mac IIcx with Adlus PageMaker 4.01, running System 7. I used my Apple LaserWriter IINT for proofing, and the final output was on a Linotronic. Main fonts used are the ITC New Baskerville and the Futura families, both from Adobe System, Inc.

Layout, design, and production by myself.

Indexed by the truly wonderful Mary Grady.

Linotronic output by my dear friend and comrade, Janet Butcher, of Desktop Composition, Petaluma.

Beautiful cover design by Ted Mader + Associates.

Just in case you wanna know

I live in Santa Rosa, California. I teach desktop design, electronic typography, and sundry other Mac classes at Santa Rosa Junior College. Janet Butcher and I also have a training business, teaching people all kinds of interesting things on the Mac, without resorting to technobabble.

Zapf Dingbats

In the chart to the left, find the Zapf Dingbat you wish to type. Hold down the Shift, the Option, or the Shift-and-Option keys while pressing the text character. The dingbat in the Zapf column needs no extra keys.

Text	Zapf	Shift	Option	Shift & Option
1	☞	✂	②	↗
2	☞	✇	♥	→
3	✓	✂	⦂	➔
4	✔	✄	⦂	→
5	✕	☎	⑤	→
6	✖	✿	♥	➡
7	✗	✆	❦	➡
8	✘	☜	♣	¶
9	✚	✈	⑥	➡
0	✎	✉	⑦	➢
-	✐	✿	⑦	⑧
=	†	☞	②	⑥
q	❑	✳	⑥	⑤
w	◗	✶	②	➢
e	❊	✧	♠	➤
r	❒	✺	♣	➡
t	▼	✳	⑨	➡
y	❘	✴	①	➡
u	◆	✳	♣	⇨
i	❋	☆	❦	④
o	❑	★	⑩	④
p	❐	☆	④	③
[	❉	❜	⑨	⑩
]	❋	❝	→	→
a	❀	✡	⎨	)
s	▲	✳	⛄	⇨
d	❅	♣	❶	⇦
f	❄	♦	⑤	⇦
g	❆	✧	♦	⇨
h	❇	★	➝	⇨
j	✼	✪	⑦	⇨
k	✳	☆	◆◆	⇨
l	●	★	③	➪
;	✛	✚	⑩	⊃
'	☯	✂	⑨	③
z	■	✲	⑧	≫➔
x	❘	✳	⑥	↘
c	❈	✛	}	(
v	❖	✳	④	↕
b	✿	✜	⑤	⊳➔
n	■	✳	❾	↗
m	○	✳	⑩	↖
,	☙	✚	⑦	➤➔
.	✐	✝	⑧	↗
/	✎	✞	↔	①
`	❀	❞	❀	→
spacebar			❶	❶
\	✳	❜	⑧	⑨

n (outlined) □   Sh-] "
l (outlined) ○   Sh- ` "
t (outlined) ▽   Sh- ['
s (outlined) △   Sh- \ ,
u (outlined) ◇
Opt-6 (outlined) ♡

Opt-Sh-/	①	Opt-u-space	①
Opt-1	②	Opt-=	②
Opt-l	③	Opt-Sh-'	③
Opt-v	④	Opt-Sh-o	④
Opt-f	⑤	Opt-5	⑤
Opt-x	⑥	Opt-Sh-=	⑥
Opt-j	⑦	Opt-,	⑦
Opt-\	⑧	Opt-.	⑧
Opt-Sh-\	⑨	Opt-y	⑨
Opt-;	⑩	Opt-m	⑩

Opt-d	❶	Opt-Spcbar	❶
Opt-w	❷	Opt-` *then* Sh-a	❷
Opt-Sh-p	❸	Opt-n *then* Sh-a	❸
Opt-p	❹	Opt-n *then* Sh-o	❹
Opt-b	❺	Opt-Sh-q	❺
Opt-q	❻	Opt-q	❻
Opt-0	❼	Opt--	❼
Opt-z	❽	Opt-Sh- -	❽
Opt-'	❾	Opt-[	❾
Opt-o	❿	Opt-Sh-[	❿

Here is a handy chart for finding some of the special characters available that will make your work look more professional

"	Option [	Opening double quote
"	Option Shift [	Closing double quote
'	Option]	Opening single quote
'	Option Shift]	Closing single quote; Apostrophe
-	Hyphen	Hyphen
–	Option Hyphen	En dash
—	Option Shift Hyphen	Em dash
…	Option ;	Ellipsis *(this character cannot be separated at the end of a line as the three periods can)*
•	Option 8	Bullet
❏	o	(in font Zapf Dingbats)
■	n	(in font Zapf Dingbats)
□	n (outlined)	(in font Zapf Dingbats)
©	Option g	Copyright symbol
™	Option 2	Trademark symbol
®	Option r	Registration symbol
°	Option Shift 8	Degree symbol: 105° F
¢	Option $	Cents symbol
/	Option Shift !	Fraction bar *(it fits fractions better and doesn't descend below the baseline as the slash does)*
fi	Option Shift 5	Ligature for **f** and **i**
fl	Option Shift 6	Ligature for **f** and **l**
£	Option 3	English pound sign
¿	Option Shift ?	Spanish symbol
ç	Option c	Cedilla, lowercase
Ç	Option Shift c	Cedilla, capital
⌘	Control Q	(only in the Chicago font; the Control key is not on a Mac Plus keyboard)

Accent Marks

Refer to page 50 to learn how to type these in; this page is merely a quick reference

´	Option e
`	Option ~
¨	Option u
~	Option n
^	Option i